# WHAT IS WALDORF EDUCATION?

# WHAT IS WALDORF EDUCATION?

THREE LECTURES BY

## RUDOLF STEINER

Introduction by

STEPHEN KEITH SAGARIN

SteinerBooks

The lectures in this volume are from the following sources: "A Lecture for Prospective Parents," August 31, 1919, in *The Spirit of the Waldorf School: Lectures Surrounding The Founding of the First Waldorf School, Stuttgart, 1919,* © 1995 by Anthroposophic Press; "The Fundamentals of Waldorf Education," November 11, 1921, in *Waldorf Education and Anthroposophy 1: Nine Public Lectures,* © 1995 by Anthroposophic Press, 1995; "Educational Issues I," August 29, 1924, in *Waldorf Education and Anthroposophy 2: Twelve Public Lectures,* © 1996 by Anthroposophic Press.

Introduction © 2003 Stephen Keith Sagarin

Published by SteinerBooks
610 Main Street, Great Barrington, MA 01230
www.steinerbooks.org

Library of Congress Cataloging-in-Publication Data
Steiner, Rudolf, 1861-1925.

[Lectures. English. Selections]

What is Waldorf education? : three lectures / by Rudolf Steiner ; introduction by Stephen Keith Sagarin.

p. cm.

Includes bibliographical references.

ISBN 0-88010-527-5

1. Waldorf method of education. 2. Anthroposophy. I. Title.

LB1029.W34S7362515 2003

371.39--dc22

2003020333

10 9 8 7 6 5 4 3 2

# Contents

# Introduction

*Recovering the Quality of Rudolf Steiner's Educational Work*

STEPHEN KEITH SAGARIN

WALDORF EDUCATION does not exist. It is not a "thing," and it cannot necessarily be distinguished from good education anywhere. Because it does not exist, it cannot be found in the boxes we call Waldorf schools. To narrow its definition to identify it with schools named Waldorf or Steiner schools, or to identify it with a particular curriculum or technique is to reify Waldorf education in a way that may describe part of what is but necessarily ignores what may also be. What we call Waldorf education may perhaps be found in any school, or anywhere that teachers teach and students learn. There is no characteristic or quality that is unique to what we call Waldorf education that cannot potentially be found somewhere else. Waldorf education, as an idea or set of ideas, slips through the cracks of any structure erected to define it.

Just as Waldorf education has no definite boundaries, it also has no definite origin. We may describe Waldorf education, for example, as arising from the educational conceptions of Rudolf Steiner. But many (most? all?) of these conceptions—for example, the idea that, culturally, at least, "ontogeny recapitulates phylogeny" (the development of an individual mirrors in microcosm the development of the species)—may be shown to be older than Steiner and therefore not to originate with him. (Beyond inferences from Steiner's work, the idea that "the" Waldorf curriculum must include Norse myths in fourth grade or Greek history in fifth grade—curricular practices common in Waldorf schools—is difficult to discover. It's not in well-known lecture cycles that he gave on education, nor is it in *The Foundations of Human Experience* and its correlates, nor may it be found in Stockmeyer's or Heydebrand's well-known descriptions of German Waldorf school curricula.) In particular, for the United States, the writings of Ralph Waldo Emerson contain in prototypical form many of Steiner's ideas about education.

### Emerson and the Waldorf Curriculum

Emerson's essay "History," for example, presents an encapsulated curriculum that mirrors closely the general curriculum of many Waldorf schools. His language, too, mirrors Steiner's in addressing the intellectual and emotional maturation of one person as, in part, a recapitulation of the intellectual and cultural developments to be found in human history.

The following quotations from "History" demonstrate the correspondence that Emerson finds between history and individual growth and development. This evolution of ideas is presumably based on knowledge of ancient cultures or at least exposure to them. Someone who had never heard of the Greeks, nor been exposed to their cultural influence even in a dilute or adulterated form, could not be expected in ontogeny to recapitulate this aspect of a cultural phylogeny. On the other hand, as Emerson implies at the end of the first two quotations, the state of being Greek, in the sense of "the spiritual nature unfolded in strict unity with the body," may be universally human even for those who do not name it by the same name as Emerson:

> What is the foundation of that interest all men feel in Greek history, letters, art and poetry, in all its periods from the Homeric age down to the domestic life of the Athenians and Spartans, four or five centuries later? What but this, that every man passes personally through a Grecian period. The Grecian state is the era of the bodily nature, the perfection of the senses—of the spiritual nature unfolded in strict unity with the body. (123)

In many Waldorf school fifth grades, when teachers claim students have achieved a grace and harmony of body and spirit that will soon be disrupted by the travails of puberty and adolescence, the class holds a Greek "Olympiad," competing for laurels in javelin, discus and running races, striving as much for form and beauty as for victory. As well, Greek myths make up a significant portion of the literature of the fifth grade in many Waldorf schools.

The comparison between Emerson's writings and Steiner's is a study in itself. One more example will suffice here. For both Steiner and Emerson, the study of nature can guide and give meaning to personal experience. Neither means by nature what we might call "environmental studies," although these would not be excluded; each means that symbolic meaning may be found in the reflective examination of the world around us.

> It is essential that the secrets of Nature, the laws of life be taught to the boy or girl, not in dry intellectual concepts, but as far as possible in symbols. Parables of the spiritual connections of things should be brought before the soul of the child in such a manner that behind the parable he

divines and feels, rather than grasps intellectually, the underlying law on all existence. "All that is passing is but a parable," must be the maxim guiding all our education in this [elementary school] period. (Steiner, 1965, 33) Here is Emerson on the same topic:

I can symbolize my thought by using the name of any creature, of any fact, because every creature is man agent or patient. Tantalus means the impossibility of drinking the waters of thought which are always gleaming and waving within sight of the soul.... Every animal of the barn-yard, the field and the forest, of the earth and the waters that are under the earth, has contrived to get a footing and to leave the print of its features and form in some one or other of these upright, heaven-facing speakers. (127)

Steiner's thinking is often prefigured in Emerson's, but this is not to say that they are the same. Toward the end of his essay "Education," Emerson (1966) tosses in a towel that Steiner held onto like a bulldog: "I confess myself utterly at a loss in suggesting particular reforms in our ways of teaching." (225) Steiner, in concert with Emil Molt and a host of others, set out to reform our ways of teaching in a myriad of concrete ways. But, while broad and systematic, few or none of these ways were as original as we might believe, nor were they meant to be particular to some schools and not others.

## A Unique Method?

Separate from the ideas in or behind Steiner's conception of education, we might describe Waldorf education as a particular method. When we define method, however—and certainly in the case of Waldorf education we are not talking about a collection of techniques or a bag of tricks, but a method in a larger sense—we omit important elements of Steiner's thinking. As Michael Lipson, recent translator of *Intuitive Thinking as a Spiritual Path*, put it, somewhat cryptically, Steiner's method is a "methodless method" that must be continually re-invented by each teacher for each student in order to be valid (Private communication, November 20, 1999). And if we use a more mundane definition of method, and speak of a particular curriculum or set of teaching techniques, Waldorf education still eludes capture. Schools that are not Waldorf schools and teachers who are not Waldorf teachers use, perhaps increasingly, techniques and conceptions of education identical to those propounded by Steiner, even though many of these teachers may never have heard Steiner's name. "Looping," in which one teacher stays with a particular class for several years, and block scheduling, in which one subject is studied intensively for a relatively brief time, are two such techniques. While no other school of which I know even approximates the curriculum found in a typical Waldorf school, there is nothing to prevent such adoption.

## The Doctor Didn't Say

One step toward recognizing that there is no such thing as Waldorf education is to realize that Rudolf Steiner himself never spoke or wrote about Waldorf education. He did speak and write at great length about education; how children grow and develop and learn, and how teachers may teach them. Further, in his work, Steiner claimed no particular originality. He did not see a discontinuity between what came before him and his own work. In his seminal pamphlet, *The Education of the Child* (1965), for example, Steiner quotes Jean Paul approvingly and at length. The sense one gets reading

Steiner's work, and this applies as well to his writings and lectures on matters other than education, is that ideas, like apples, lead an objective existence, and may be plucked by anyone. We might say that the "method" of Waldorf education is to learn to pluck these apples for oneself, as student or teacher, and not to rely on the authority of Rudolf Steiner to hand one already-picked apples. The analogy holds in that we may no more reify Waldorf education than we may divorce apples from the tree, sun, soil of their birth. Ideas, like apples, exist in and arise out of a context.

## Staking a Claim

While I dispute the existence of "Waldorf" education, I do not dispute the existence of a group of schools that have chosen to identify themselves with the first Waldorf school in Stuttgart by calling themselves Waldorf schools, or to identify themselves with statements about education made by Rudolf Steiner by calling themselves Steiner schools. These schools have had a life of their own for more than seventy years in the United States, and have made a powerful claim on the ideas lumped under the term "Waldorf education."

I cannot define or describe Waldorf education well, but I can investigate how others have defined or described it. I will begin outside the United States to include some of what Steiner himself said about what we now call Waldorf education. I will then focus on the strategies that writers and teachers in the United States have used to write about Waldorf education. (To see how Steiner's conceptions of education made their way from Germany and Switzerland to the United States, see Ida Oberman's study, 1999. Not available, unfortunately, is a similar account of the influence of British Waldorf schools and teachers on the United States. This is a study waiting to be written.)

## Compromise

> Moreover, I should like to point out to you that the real aim and object of our education is not to found as many schools as possible... but our education concerns itself with methods of teaching, and it is essentially a new way and art of education, so all teachers can bring it into their work in whatever kind of school they happen to be... and I have declared that the methods can be introduced into every situation where someone has the good will to do it.
> (Attributed to Rudolf Steiner; reference uncertain)

Some will acknowledge the validity of this passage but insist on a distinction between those who employ a "compromised" version of Steiner's method ("Waldorf-inspired" schools or teachers) and "real" Waldorf schools that have deliberately dedicated themselves to this method. I maintain, however, that all manifestations of Rudolf Steiner's educational ideas are necessarily compromised. Schools that see themselves as pure because they are independent of the potentially corrupting influence of government money may be compared with schools, like the Milwaukee Urban Waldorf School, a choice school within the Milwaukee public school system, that have made overt compromises to meet present requirements regarding the separation of church and state. (One of these compromises has been to eliminate the word "God" from a verse that children in the school say each morning.) The Milwaukee school's compromise is a deliberate choice made to facilitate other educational objectives, especially the education of relatively poor urban children. Independent (non-public) Waldorf schools, on the other hand, have clearly chosen, if not so deliberately, not to serve poor and near-poor students like those who attend the Milwaukee school. This choice is also a compromise.

## Three of a Kind: Strategies and Descriptions

*A First Strategy: Waldorf Schools ARE Waldorf Education*

Existing descriptions of Waldorf education can be characterized according to three strategies. The first and simplest is to let Waldorf schools stand for a description; what goes on in Waldorf schools is inferred to be, by definition, Waldorf education. Ida Oberman's otherwise excellent history, *Fidelity and Flexibility in Waldorf Education, 1919-1998,* slips into this mode, examining the histories of Waldorf schools in Germany and the United States, implying that these add up to a larger history of Waldorf education. To further her discussion she uses the concept of a "cultural field," a metaphorical container for Waldorf education. Just as the field is a metaphor, so too is Waldorf education.

Stephen Talbott also uses this first strategy in an appendix to the also otherwise excellent book *The Future Does Not Compute.* He asks, "What is Waldorf Education?" and answers with a description of the founding of the first school and a description of a generalized curriculum. (424)

If Waldorf education were a consistent and prescribed method and curriculum, these analogies might suffice—although their definition is circular. But what goes on in Waldorf schools varies from place to place and time to time. There is no single characteristic, in fact, without which a Waldorf school cannot exist, nor that defines a school as a Waldorf school. Mentally erase beeswax crayons, or a eurythmist, or even the morning verse. A school without these items could still fulfill Steiner's wishes for the education of children, I believe. Waldorf education simply cannot be seen as the accumulation or collection of some (even infinite) number of defining characteristics. To indulge such a fragmented view is to give credence to a reductionism that Waldorf education stands against.

## *A Second Strategy: Pigeonholes*

The second strategy is to pigeonhole Waldorf education according to some cultural or historical characteristic that, while real enough within a particular context, may not be necessary or sufficient to describe something larger called Waldorf education. Waldorf education is defined only partially if it is defined as a reform movement, for example. To the extent that authors acknowledge the contingency of such synecdochical definitions (definitions in which the part stands for the whole), they may be serviceable, if incomplete.

### Henry Barnes and the Movement

Henry Barnes, author and long-time history teacher and faculty chairman at the Rudolf Steiner School in New York City, characterizes Waldorf education as a particular movement: "As one of the most rapidly growing yet least known independent, nonsectarian school movements in the free world today, Rudolf Steiner or Waldorf education should be brought to the attention of all serious students of education." (323) This may be true, but Waldorf education is only "independent" [of public education in the United States] and only a "movement" in the here and now.

Barnes writes, "This article will briefly outline the history of the Waldorf movement and seek to give an introduction to the philosophy and methods that underlie it." (323) Philosophy and methods sound promising; they may extend beyond consideration of Waldorf education as a movement. For Barnes, the philosophy is based on two major principles or insights. The primary or defining principle of Waldorf education is an image of the human being:

Behind the Waldorf curriculum, its methods of instruction, and all the many practical aspects one thinks of when one thinks of a Waldorf school today stands the idea of man and of child development from which they all spring. It is this idea that gives them meaning and, in the end, is the basis on which the [Waldorf education] movement will have to be evaluated and judged. (326)

To speak of the education of a child necessarily implies a concept of what or who this child is. Historical examples abound, including Locke's "tabula rasa," Rousseau's good "natural man" Emile, Jonathan Edwards' very different "natural man" in original sin, and Dewey's concept of the child in community. For Barnes, Waldorf schools attempt to educate according to Rudolf Steiner's image of a human being:

In Steiner's view, the human being can never be fully understood in terms of his heredity and the impact of his environment. Beyond them lies the essential core of human individuality, which cannot be defined in material terms. That central entity, the human ego, is perceived by Steiner to be supersensible and eternal, revealing itself by reflection in the personality who is active here in time and space. It is the educator's responsibility to help this personality to develop in such a way that it can become a fitting vehicle through which the real ego can express itself. (326)

Note that Barnes refers to "educators" in the last sentence that was quoted, not to "Waldorf educators." The virtual brand name "Waldorf" is a label attached after Steiner, not by Steiner. The label "Waldorf" represents an increasing objectification of ideas that were initially less defined and therefore more open to play and experiment than they often seem.

The words "in Steiner's view" and "perceived by Steiner" are almost extraneous here. Steiner is certainly not the only nor the first person to speak of a human being as more than the sum of genes and environment. If he, and others who find the world this way, are correct, then inferences regarding education follow not from authority but from a perceived reality. Where reference to Steiner should be inserted in the quotation above is in the last sentence. "[For Steiner,] it is the educator's responsibility...." Even here, Steiner is not unique, although his lectures and writings certainly constitute the most thorough and systematic approach to education from this perspective.

Barnes' point is that the "supersensible and eternal" incarnate in the world, according to Steiner, gradually and in a specific fashion. Education, therefore, should be conducted in accordance with what is known about this process of incarnation. Hence, the methods and curricula derive from this view.

For Barnes, a second principle grows from the first; because the human self is seen to incarnate over a period of years, education must address this development, which is seen to occur in three broad stages lasting roughly seven years each. (Many writers on Waldorf education treat these as if they were universal, when Steiner himself made it clear time and again that he was describing something that was historically and culturally true, not true everywhere and for all time.) The method and curriculum similarly derive from these principles, and provide the particulars visible to any visitor to a Waldorf school, including instructional materials and subject matter. These will likely include relatively featureless rag dolls, beeswax crayons, watercolor paints, colored chalk, stories of Christian saints, Norse and Greek Myths, and any number of other things. But the rhetorical question still begs, does any of these make a Waldorf school?

Barnes's consideration of methods and philosophy extends his definition beyond the merely synecdochical, but his discussion here speaks best to education in general, not to "Waldorf" education. This supports my contention that there is no such thing as Waldorf education.

## Oberman's Objectification

Ida Oberman's history of Waldorf education also offers an objectified view. For her, "Waldorf" is a "unique" "German" "progressive" "alternative" "reform initiative" or "institution" which has "embedded" in it "an ideology, a belief system called Anthroposophy." All of these descriptions may apply to "Waldorf education," but each could change radically without disturbing Steiner's contributions to ways of teaching.

Oberman locates sources for the curriculum of the first Waldorf school in Steiner's intellectual biography, but, having shown its somewhat contingent nature, then treats it as an object to be relocated wherever "Waldorf" roots. Oberman shows how different people—Hermann von Baravalle, Marie Steiner and Ita Wegman—and different schools—the Rudolf Steiner School in New York City, the Kimberton Waldorf School, and the Sacramento Waldorf School—adopt different strategies ("purity," "accommodation," and "evolution"), but not how curricula reflect their origins in Steiner's work and in the time and place of their implementation.

Among the evidence for this point of view is Oberman's insertion of the bracketed qualifier "Waldorf" into a quotation in which it did not formerly appear: "The faculty now active at the school have proven ... their willingness to continue this [Waldorf] work, which represents the noblest of German cultural life for all to see." (1999. Emil Molt and Duke Fritz von Bothmer, p. 134) It is clear that Oberman sees the work as "Waldorf" work, but this is her own objectification.

## A Third Strategy: School Functions

A third strategy involves some function or group of functions that Waldorf education performs (is claimed to perform).

If the difficulty of the last definition is that it is too narrow—what is does not define what else may be—the difficulty of a functional definition is that it is too broad. Good education of any kind will necessarily perform certain functions that cannot simply be claimed for, let's say, Waldorf education. Waldorf teachers are not the only teachers to claim a developmental view of their students, nor the only to find some aspects of human individuality that cannot be attributed solely to the interaction of heredity and the environment. Further, it does not appear that there is some unique set of functions that only something called Waldorf education performs.

### Eugene Schwartz's Functionalism

For Eugene Schwartz, Waldorf education is a method, based on the work of Rudolf Steiner, who "begins with a qualitative intelligence that is unitary and suggests that the task of education is to multiply it. If [Howard] Gardner's theory concerns itself with 'multiple intelligences,' then Steiner's approach might be called 'intelligent multiplicity.'" (151)

Further, Schwartz describes Waldorf education as a "'will first' pedagogy" or "methodology" that aims to "educate the child in accordance with principles that ask us to honor and work with the soul and spiritual nature of the youngster." (157) While this sounds vague, it is only his introduction into a more specific examination of methods and techniques that teachers may use.

As for setting these ideas in a context as large as that of Barnes or Curran (see below), I don't believe Schwartz sees this as a helpful goal; his more immediately practical goal is to show how Waldorf education can function to address the needs of children in a particular place and time. That is, he is concerned with the "will" education of children in wealthy industrialized countries.

## A Look at the Map

Eugene Schwartz also approaches the function of Waldorf education by analogy. Like a map, Schwartz posits, a curriculum can be understood on three levels. The first, a global, geophysical map, remains valid for centuries. For Schwartz, Steiner's description of child development is such a durable aspect of Waldorf education. Development itself may change, but only slowly. School subjects—history, math, and so forth—change more rapidly, and have been modified significantly over the decades since Waldorf education began. These are akin to a political map, which may change more rapidly. An up-to-date road map, however, must "come alive every day." The clear advantage of Schwartz' analogy is that it neatly allows for both relatively unchanging and continually changing aspects of Waldorf education. One danger of this view, however, is that agreement on the unchanging aspects of the map may be perceived as dogma—unchanging and therefore unquestioned. The history of geology shows, however, that while the earth appears to change slowly, our views and interpretations of that change can be revised radically from one year to the next. The notion that Waldorf education is a thing, however immaterial, has developed so surreptitiously over the past decades that we have not noticed the change. Our map has not changed much, perhaps, but we may be in danger of mistaking the map for the thing itself.

## A Quality of Education

Each of the strategies outlined above makes Waldorf education into a thing, whether a material thing like a school, or an ideological thing like a movement, or a mental thing like a function. Not all writers on Waldorf education, however, resort to these three strategies. Those who perceive Waldorf education not as a thing but as a quality of education demonstrate a different possibility for description.

## Peter Curran on Waldorf Education

Peter Curran, graduate of Bowdoin College and long-time history teacher at The Waldorf School of Garden City, adopts a strategy similar to Barnes's in describing Waldorf education, but then ventilates it immediately to include, potentially, all schools, not a particular subset. Following his retirement in the late 1980s, Curran set down some of his ideas about Waldorf schools. Particularly, he believed that there were four "essentials," "without which no school (by whatever name) is a Waldorf School and with which any school is a Waldorf School."

I. …As each child's consciousness matures, it recapitulates the cultural epochs of all Mankind. Waldorf education agrees with Emerson when he says that all children go through a Greek period and a Roman period, etc. There is, then, a proper time and method for particular subjects to be taught.

II. Since no one destroys what one loves, reverence, awe and respect for the Earth should be fostered. An inkling of the spirituality of the Earth then comes into being.

III. The qualitative, as well as the quantitative, in all things should be equally developed.

IV. Above all, Man is known as a spiritual as well as a physical being.

Curran's statement poses a realism to Barnes's nominalism in that the enactment of these principles does not depend on the presence or absence of the name "Waldorf."

Of Curran's four principles, the first and last are potentially controversial, while the middle two may be found in many classrooms and schools. The first, the "ontogeny recapitulates phylogeny" statement, is probably the least familiar to most educators, and it may be the most dated, arising out of Aristotle's "Great Chain of Being." (See, for example, Lovejoy, 1936 and 1964) Few, if any, schools other than Waldorf schools today organize themselves around such a principle. Still, there is nothing to prevent them doing so if they choose. (Nor, if Waldorf schools found a different central metaphor, would they necessarily cease to be good schools.)

Last, some contemporary interpretations of the anti-establishment of religion clause of the First Amendment to the U.S. Constitution might prevent Curran's fourth principle from being overtly applied in public schools, but the concept is hardly unique among independent schools. Some Waldorf teachers may argue that principle four may be found in many schools, but that Waldorf schools mean something different by "spirit." I'm not convinced of this, however, and, in any event, it needn't be so.

### Douglas Sloan's "Education of the Imagination"

Douglas Sloan, retired Professor of History and Education at Teachers College, NY, worked diligently through writing and teaching to present an open-minded approach to Waldorf education. In *Insight-Imagination,* he describes Waldorf education sensitively in his discussion of a larger "education of the imagination." (211)

Maurice Merleau-Ponty (1964) wrote of the "primacy of perception": "all consciousness is perceptual, even the consciousness of ourselves…. The perceived world is the always presupposed foundation of all rationality, all value and all existence." (13) For Sloan, the faculty of "imagination" necessarily accompanies perception, without which we would live in William James' "buzzing, blooming confusion." For Sloan, imagination is not simply one faculty among others—empathy or cognition, say—to be strengthened through an enhanced curriculum. Imagination is the necessary wellspring of human experience of the world:

> ... it is only through imagination that we have any knowledge whatsoever.... The imagination, the image-making power of the mind ... shapes our everyday perception of the world, for there is no perception separate from interpretation. (140)

Similarly to Barnes, Sloan describes Waldorf education according to a conception of educational stages. After briefly examining Piaget with regard to stages, however, Sloan qualifies his statements: "Any conception of educational stages must... stand constantly ready to be reevaluated and revised in the light of new evidence from any field of research...." (212) For Sloan, Waldorf education does not approach a faith, nor was it created ready-made by Rudolf Steiner, to be preserved in perpetuity like a Colonial reenactment. "Such a conception of education must as a whole remain open and subject to revision...." (212) Waldorf education is an evolving model of educational thinking, research and practice, and must be created anew in each application if it is not to devolve into prescription or dogma.

### Nancy Parsons Whittaker's Open Door Policy

Nancy Parsons Whittaker is a translator of Steiner's work into English and a founder and administrator of www.bob-nancy.com, a website devoted to Waldorf education. The paragraphs that follow do not set forth a thing-like definition, but attempt to throw open the doors of a somewhat cloistered "movement":

> I believe that the educational movement Steiner founded drifted very far from its source the moment [the act of] founding schools became more important than examining the quality of education the children were receiving and working to really convey the approach to other teachers in all manner of schools and situations. What we call "Waldorf Education" has largely come to mean a set of curricula and specific ways of introducing specific subject matter. This has nothing (in my opinion) to do with the original intent, which was to convey the attitude, the viewpoint toward the children and toward society (any society) with which a teacher could fully meet the physical, mental and spiritual needs of both the students and their community.

> Any school is a Waldorf school if the intent of Steiner's pedagogy is being met within its halls. What was the intent? The intent was to offer an education in a way that gave each child a fundamental, true introduction into the foundation of his or her society while at the same time enhancing that child's ability to accurately perceive life around him or her without damaging the child's innate capacity to be sensitively aware of the Creative Love behind the visible world (whatever that capacity might have been, whether large, small or nearly nonexistent—the teaching was not intended to train a student's spiritual vision, just not to damage what already existed). The education was not intended to found schools separated from their society at large nor was it intended to model a particular belief system.

These goals can be met in a wide variety of settings, with an infinitely wide possibility of curricula, through the myriad possibilities of human personality.

## A Necessary Lack of Definition

I used to have a bumper sticker that read "Waldorf Education" on two lines, "Waldorf" above and "Education" below. I returned to long-term parking after a research trip to discover that someone had neatly sliced off the word "Waldorf," who knows why, leaving a narrow bumper sticker that read simply: "Education." I started to remove it but stopped. It's still on my car.

Those who aim deliberately not to objectify Waldorf education can avoid the pitfalls of reification, synecdoche, or function. These writers necessarily leave Waldorf education undefined, and characterize it in refreshingly open terms. Waldorf education becomes not a thing, not a kind or brand of education, but a quality of education. And qualities, like colors, like the warmth of a heart, may expand boundlessly.

## Introduction to the Lectures

Given my assertion that Waldorf education is not a "thing," how are we to read the following introductory lectures? We chose the lectures reprinted in this volume for their broad appeal and for the degree to which they illuminate Rudolf Steiner's view of the mission and place of education—not necessarily labeled "Waldorf"—in society and for the individual, especially as these are connected with the founding of the first Waldorf school in Stuttgart in 1919. By extension, these lectures can give an overview and understanding of what occurs—or should occur—in Waldorf schools. We chose the lectures, as well, with an eye to the English-speaking reader who has an interest in a direct and accessible investigation of Steiner's vision of teaching and learning.

In the first lecture of this volume, Steiner emphasizes the role of education in "restructuring human social relations." In the second, he is concerned more with "the individual treatment of each child even within a large class." For those concerned to know whether education for Steiner is more community-oriented (are there possible links with John Dewey's idea of democracy as conjoint community and schools as proto-communities?) or more individually oriented (are there possible links with Piagetian ideas of individual development?), the answer is both and neither.

Steiner's monism, his view that matter and spirit are revelations of each other (although not equal and opposite), considers the individual as the necessary moral center for society and society as the framework for the education of the individual. Steiner maintains the healthy tension between individual and society as a necessary description of life without privileging one over the other.

Steiner makes clear in these few lectures, as he also does elsewhere, that Waldorf schools are not opposed to conventional systems of education, they do not offer a "plan for reform" (p. 101), and they are not ideological or dogmatic. Waldorf schools, however, have attracted their critics. These claim, for example, that the schools are ideological or dogmatic to the point, if they are chartered within a public system, of violating the principle of separation of church and state. Is anthroposophy—Steiner's name for his method of investigating the place of human beings in the world—a religion? The best simple response comes from Dorothy St. Charles (1994), former Principal of the Milwaukee Urban Waldorf School, the only non-charter public Waldorf (or Waldorf-inspired) school in the U.S: "Some people make it one."

A related question concerns the relationship between Steiner's ideas about education and his ideas about knowledge and the world; that is, between Waldorf education and anthroposophy or spiritual science. Steiner has this to say about that relationship:

> Education can only be based on a knowledge of the human being. It can be fruitful only if one doesn't separate theory from practice, and if, instead, knowledge passes into activity, as in the case of a true artist, into creative activity. It can bear fruit only if all knowledge is art—if, instead of being a science, educational science becomes art, the art of education. Such an active form of knowledge of the human being must then become the basis of all educational work.

> This is why there is an anthroposophical pedagogy at all. Not because certain people are fanatics of anthroposophy, thinking of it as some "jack of all trades" that can do everything, and therefore, among other things, can also educate children! Anthroposophical pedagogy exists because it is inherently necessary. An art of education can grow only from a realistic, mature knowledge of the human being, the knowledge that anthroposophy attempts to provide. This is why we have an anthroposophical art of education. (1996, 111)

Anthroposophy, I should point out, exists in the two forms in which we find every science—as a method of investigation and as the collected results of this investigation. Anthroposophy itself also has at least two meanings. The most general is illuminated by its etymology, "human wisdom." Just as someone who is not trained as a psychologist may have valid psychological insights, so someone who has never heard the word anthroposophy may have—is likely to have—insights that may be called part of the wisdom of humanity. In its more specific meaning, anthroposophy refers to the spiritual exercises that Steiner outlined in, for example, *How to Know Higher Worlds*, and to systematic descriptions of spiritual worlds and their relationship to the naively-understood world in which we find ourselves. This study and its extrapolation into practice were the lifework of Rudolf Steiner. There is a clear tension between these two meanings and these two understandings— one broad and inclusive, the other deep and exclusive. A necessary ambiguity obtains among these descriptions. When Steiner uses the word "anthroposophy," the meaning depends on the context in which it is used. Still, it is clear that there is no possible separation between Waldorf education as a humanizing education and anthroposophy as the ground for Steiner's description of human beings and knowledge.

What characterizes Waldorf schools, then? They aim at a new system of education, a practical method—but not "a few abstract rules" (p. 59). For Waldorf schools, an anthroposophical perspective "becomes a means of orientation" (p. 62) for teachers, who must develop "a kind of refined, practical instinct for action" (p. 70). According to Steiner, this practice leads to "a new kind of love," "real love" (p. 43–44), which assists teachers in protecting students "from inner impediments and hindrances [to freedom]" (p. 106). Steiner makes the claim, at once obvious and profound, that students who are educated by teachers imbued with love, with inspiration, with enthusiasm for their work, learn more easily and more quickly than those who are not. Readers interested in a practical instinct for action or in developing a new kind of love may be interested in Steiner's *Intuitive Thinking As a Spiritual Path* (also published as *Philosophy of Freedom*) or *How to Know*

*Higher Worlds* (also published as *Knowledge of Higher Worlds and Its Attainment*).

Many readers of these lectures will likely be parents at Waldorf schools. Steiner is clear that his ideas only flourish with the support of all involved. "It would be something beautiful for you [parents] to say with heartfelt meaning, 'We want to be pioneers for a future educational system. We want to be pioneers in the sense that we want to be the first to entrust our children to such an educational system of the future, one working for a new social life.'" (p. 46) He does not intend, however, for this support to be unconditional: "The people who have the most reason to hope for an improvement of conditions prevailing in contemporary education are the parents, and they, above all, have the right to expect and demand something better from the teachers." (p. 84)

Reading Steiner's lectures, when we have a healthy interest in what we're reading, often gives us the feeling that we already know what he is saying. His writing is free of jargon or terminology (with the exception of terms such as "etheric" and "astral," used to describe immaterial attributes of human existence, terms he explains carefully in the third lecture in this volume), using common words in a manner that allows us to see new connections among concepts we hold already. Re-reading Steiner's lectures over years, however, we realize that obvious revelations they contain now were invisible to us previously. Although the language is transparent, the understandings it contains are profound. They reveal themselves to us when we are capable of grasping them.

One term not elucidated in the lectures deserves a note. "Spiritual science," Steiner's descriptive term for anthroposophy, his study of the place of human beings in the world, is a more common term in Germany than it is in the English-speaking world. Open a university catalog in Germany, and you will find the term *Geisteswissenschaft*, "spiritual science," used to describe courses in what English speakers call the humanities. Studies that concern quality over quantity, we might say, are "spiritual sciences." They may be profound, but nothing mystical is meant by the term.

The lectures in this book are chosen to span Steiner's time with the Waldorf School. The first was given on the first day of a celebration opening the school. The second was given almost two years later, and the third was given just months before Steiner's death.

These lectures were given to a variety of audiences, as well. The first was addressed to prospective parents at the first Waldorf school, the second to a general German-speaking audience, and the third to English educators. Readers may note a difference in the lectures as Steiner adapts his presentation for his audience, particularly when he moves beyond his native German culture to address an English-speaking audience more akin to our own.

Steiner uses many more examples, for instance, when speaking to the English than he does when speaking to Germans. I believe he understood the consciousness of English-speakers to respond to a more practical mode of expression. Similarly, he altogether avoids use of the unfamiliar terms "etheric" and "astral." I believe, here, too, he found English speakers had little patience for such terminology, and preferred explanations in more familiar words. Both of these characteristics of this lecture point toward differences between a German or central European mode of expression and an English-speaking mode, something Steiner aimed to accommodate in lectures to English speakers. (When speaking in England, Steiner lectured in German, and a native English speaker translated immediately afterward. The translation printed here is taken from a shorthand transcription of the German.)

The stylistic difference between Steiner's German and English lectures is worth noting for two reasons. The first is the difficulty English speakers may have in engaging with Steiner's work in general. This cultural difficulty may be overcome by careful reading and a willingness to supply our own examples where Steiner does not (hence one great value of a study group or reading group; several people can temper predilections or misunderstandings that might slide past an individual). This is hard work, but rewarding.

The second reason is that this perceived difference between German and English cultures may have influenced the growth of Waldorf schools in the United States, especially through the activity of Hermann von Baravalle, who has been called the "Johnny Appleseed" of Waldorf schools in the United States. Baravalle was a teacher at the first Waldorf School in Stuttgart who moved to the United States and was connected with almost all the Waldorf schools founded here between 1928 and 1959. He lectured, advised or taught at the Rudolf Steiner School, NY, the High Mowing School, NH, the Kimberton Farm School, PA, the Waldorf School of Garden City, NY, the Green Meadow Waldorf School, NY, the Highland Hall School, CA, and the Sacramento Waldorf School, CA, among others. To our point, he believed strongly that Americans were unreceptive to the more esoteric, less immediately practical aspects of Steiner's educational work. He deliberately excised passages from translations of Steiner's lectures and refrained in lectures from mentioning even anthroposophy (although he credited Steiner as a great thinker and a practical man). Some anthroposophists believed he went too far in this regard; when parents later "discovered" Steiner's esotericism, they believed something had been withheld from them. And it had. On the other hand, Baravalle's success in promoting the growth of Waldorf schools in the U.S. is unparalleled. It is likely, in any event, that Baravalle's behavior grew out of an understanding that he shared with Steiner—Baravalle was "accredited" by Steiner to give public lectures on anthroposophy—regarding English and American modes of understanding.

To a lesser degree, we chose the lectures here because they contain relatively few references to other, particularly German, writers and scientists. Many of Steiner's public lectures on education, for example, aimed to situate his ideas in the context of the thinking of his day, and they contain considerations of Herbart, Dubois-Reymond, and others. These names may be familiar to some, but they hardly hold the floor in contemporary debates about topics such as education, freedom, or materialism. It is useful to translate their ideas into modern idioms, but this exercise would stretch the purpose of the present volume too far. Suffice to say that there were those who proposed ideas about education that supported or conflicted with Steiner's ideas then, and there are those today whose ideas may do likewise.

Finally, we deliberately did not choose lectures that Steiner delivered in training teachers; that is not our aim in this introductory volume. Those who are interested in pursuing readings in Steiner's teacher training might first read *The Education of the Child in the Light of Anthroposophy* (also published as *The Education of the Child in the Light of Spiritual Science*), and then the lectures Steiner gave to the first teachers in the Waldorf School and the concurrent discussions he had with them: *Foundations of Human Experience*, *Practical Advice for Teachers*, and *Discussions With Teachers*. These are followed by several other courses of lectures.

## Conclusion

Steiner relates the following anecdote in the middle lecture of this small collection: "Whenever I come to Stuttgart to visit and assist in the guidance of the school, I ask the same question in each class, naturally within the appropriate context and avoiding any possible tedium, 'Children, do you love your teachers?' You should hear and witness the enthusiasm with which they call out in chorus, 'Yes!' This call to the teachers to engender love within their pupils is all part of the question of how the older generation should relate to the young." (p. 90)

We are all older than some and younger than others; we learn from some and we teach others. If we foster the relationship Steiner describes here, then we participate in an education that honors the memory of Rudolf Steiner.

REFERENCES

Barnes, H. (1980) An introduction to waldorf education. In *Teachers College Record,* 81 (3), Spring 1980; pp. 322-336.

Curran, P. (1990) Unpublished typescript.

Emerson, R. (1966) Education. In *Emerson on education: Selections,* H. Jones (Ed.). Teachers College Press: New York.

Lovejoy, A. (1936 and 1964) *The great chain of being: A study of the history of an idea.* Harvard University Press: Cambridge, MA.

Merleau-Ponty, M. (1964) *The primacy of perception and other essays on phenomenological psychology, the philosophy of art, history and politics,* J. Edie (Ed.) Northwestern University Press: Chicago.

Oberman, I. (1999) *Fidelity and flexibility in Waldorf education, 1919-1998.* UMI Dissertation Services: Ann Arbor.

St. Charles, Dorothy, interview by Alan Chartock, WAMC radio, 90.3 FM, Albany, NY, April 1994.

Schwartz, E. (1999) *Millennial child: Transforming education in the twenty-first century.* Anthroposophic Press: Hudson, NY.

Sloan, D. (1983) *Insight-Imagination: The emancipation of thought and the modern world.* Greenwood Publishing: Westport, CT.

Steiner, R. (1965) *The education of the child in the light of anthroposophy,* G. & M. Adams (Trans.) Rudolf Steiner Press: New York.

Steiner, R. (1996) Why base education on anthroposophy? June 30, 1923. In *Waldorf Education and Anthroposophy 2: Twelve Public Lectures.* Anthroposophic Press: Hudson, NY.

Talbott, S. (1995) *The Future Does Not Compute: Transcending The Machines in our Midst.* O'Reilly and Associates: Sebastopol, CA.

Whittaker, N. (2001) Post to subscribers of the list server Waldorf@maelstrom.stjohns.edu., Feb. 11. Subscribe at http://www.bobnancy.com. Quoted with author's permission.

---

Stephen Keith Sagarin is Faculty Administrator and teacher at the Great Barrington Rudolf Steiner School, MA; Director of the M.S.Ed. Program in Waldorf Teacher Training at Sunbridge College, NY; and adjunct faculty in history and education in the Department of Organization and Leadership, Teachers College, NY. He has an A.B. in art history and fine art from Princeton University and a Ph.D. in history and education from Columbia University. He has been a Waldorf teacher for most of his career, including eleven years at the Waldorf School of Garden City, the high school from which he graduated.

# 1

# A Lecture for Prospective Parents

WHEN MR. MOLT first set out to found a school for the children of his employees, clearly his intention was to serve humanity in these difficult times. He chose a means that we must employ above all others when working to heal our social conditions. It is written in all your souls that we must create something new out of the conditions that we experience— the conditions that have developed over the past three or four centuries in the so-called civilized world. It must also have been deeply written in your souls that what we need above all to achieve other conditions is a different way of preparing human beings for a place in the world, through upbringing and education. What we need is a way untainted by the traditions of the past three or four centuries that are now reaching their zenith.

· For the future, we expect a social structure much different from the one of the present. We have a right to expect that. We look lovingly at our children, at the next generation, and we, particularly those who are parents, often have misgivings in our hearts. How will our loved ones fit into a society that must be so different from that of the present? Will they be equal to the new social challenge coming to humanity? Will they be capable of contributing to the formation of society, so that those who come after us will have it other than we have had, will have, in a much different sense, a more humane existence than we have had?

Everyone feels that the question of upbringing and education is, in a profound sense, a question of the highest order. This is particularly true in times like ours, times of sudden change and transformation of society. We look back at the terrible times humanity has recently lived through in Europe, we look upon the rivers of blood that have flowed, and we see the great army of unhappy people, their bodies broken and their souls shattered, which necessarily resulted from the unnatural conditions of recent times. When we look upon all this, the desire wells up in us to ask, "In the broadest sense, how must we bring up people so that this will be impossible in the future?" Out of this privation and misery, an understanding must awaken for the role of education in restructuring human social relations.

In principle, we hear this expressed from many sides. Yet, we must ask ourselves, when people say this here and there, if they always mean it in the correct sense. Today, people say pleasant words about many things. These pleasant words do not always arise from inner strength, nor above all else, from inner truths that can put into practice the content of these words. Today those people who are called upon to school and educate our children come forth, offer their opinions and notions, and say, "We know how children should be brought up and educated. We should simply do it just as we have always wanted, but have not been allowed to do—then the right thing will occur." Behind those who so speak, we hear those who feel themselves called to teach the teachers. They assure us, "We have the right views about what teachers should become. Just follow us. We will send the right teachers into the world, so everything goes well in education." Yet, when we look deeply into what has become of our social conditions, we want to shout to both these teachers and these teachers of teachers, "You may mean well, but you do not really know what you are talking about!" For nothing can help modern education, nothing can raise modern education to a better state, unless the teachers admit, "We come from the traditions formed during the past three or four centuries. We were trained in the way that leads humanity into such misfortune." In their turn, those who trained the teachers must admit, "We have not understood anything except how to give teachers the results of industrialism, statism, capitalism. Of course, we have delivered the present teachers, who fit into this present social configuration, this configuration that simply must change."

This means that, just as we demand a change, a transformation of the full spectrum of the present social structure for the future, we must also demand another art of education, and a different basis for this art!

In many respects, the question of education today is a question of teachers. Today, when we speak with those who want to become teachers and educators, we frequently sense the deep antisocial feeling lying within humanity. We speak with them about what education should become in the future. They say, "Yes, I have been saying that all along. We should raise children to be competent modern-day people. We should educate them to be useful people. We should not pay so much attention to vocational training, but more to the training of the whole person." They talk about such things and go away with the impression that they think just the same as we think. They think just the opposite!

Today, our antisocial life has come so far that people express opposites with the same words. This is what makes it so difficult to understand one another. Someone who truly thinks socially, thinks very differently from modern people satisfied with the old traditions. In the same way, we must think fundamentally differently about teaching and education when we attempt to solve the educational social question in a particular instance. We must think differently from those who believe we can base this change on their traditional educational methods. Truly, today we must think and perceive more thoroughly than many believe. In addition, we must be clear that we cannot create something new out of the old educational and scientific methods; education and science must themselves change.

This is adequate justification for us to begin this work of starting the Waldorf school with a course for the faculty. We have attempted to select for the faculty people who, at the least, are rooted in the old educational system to a greater or lesser degree—for one it is more, for another less. But, we were also intent on finding people who have the heart and soul for the reconstruction of our society and culture. We sought people who have the heart and soul for what it means to raise the children of today to be the people of tomorrow.

Our new teachers also must carry another conviction in their souls, namely, that from the time children enter school we may teach them only what the essence of humanity dictates. In this sense we want to found a unified school in the truest sense of the word. All we want to know in the growing child is the developing human being. We want to learn from the nature of the developing child how children want to develop themselves as human beings, that is, how their nature, their essence should develop to become truly human.

"That is just what we also want," the old teachers and educators of teachers tell us. "We have always tried to teach people, to consider, for example, the distinct personalities of the children."

Yes, we must reply, you have striven to train children to be what you perceived human beings to be, the kind of people you thought were necessary for the old political and economic life. We cannot do anything with this idea of "human beings"; and the future of humanity will not know what to do with it nor want to know. We need a fundamental renewal.

The first thing needed for the educational system of the future is a new understanding of humanity. The understanding of humanity that has swollen up out of the morass of materialism in the last centuries and has been dressed up in our higher schools of learning as the basis of human nature cannot be the basis of the art of education in the future. What we require is a new perception of human nature. We can derive this only from a new science. The science taught today, and also represented by those who teach, is only the reflection of older times. Just as a new epoch should come, so too should come a new science, a new way to train teachers, a new pedagogy built upon a new understanding of human beings. For just that reason, we pay particular attention to a real understanding of humanity in the course to prepare the faculty for the Waldorf school. We cherish the hope that the future teachers in the Waldorf school will come to know the developing human. We hope that they will give this embryonic human the capacities that the future will require of people who work in the socially formed human society. We sense that much of what the old way of teaching has said about humanity is just words. Today we study the true essence of human thought, so we can train the child in the right kind of thinking. We study the true basis of real human feeling, so that in the genuinely social community people bring forth justice based upon true human feeling. We study the essence of human will, so that this human will can embrace and permeate the newly formed economic life of the future. We do not study people in a materialistic, one-sided way; we study the body, soul and spirit of the human being, so that our teachers can train the body, soul and spirit of human beings. We do not speak of body, soul and spirit merely as words. We attempt to discover how the various stages of the human being result from one another. We look carefully at how the children are when they enter the school, and the faculty takes over from the parents.

How superficially the so-called educational sciences have observed this period of human growth! There is an important turning point in the life of a child; it lies around the age of seven, just about that year in which the child enters elementary school. It is just at that year when the teacher should take over the child from the parents for a portion of the further education. The external expression of this important period of life is the change of teeth; however, the new teeth are only an outward sign of the important change occurring within.

Certainly, you have already heard much about what we need to understand to properly comprehend social reforms, and so forth. However, many of you were probably still of the opinion, received from a study by the leading experts, that everything has already been taken care of for humanity in an admirable way. The most important things have not been done! Modern people find it quite strange, when we say that at the age when the child enters school, an inner revolution occurs in the human soul, in the whole being, which is only outwardly expressed only in the cutting of teeth. Until that time children are imitating beings, beings that bring through birth the urge to do everything as it is done around them. In these first years it is simply a part of human nature to allow ourselves to be trained by what we see in our surroundings. Just at the time of the cutting of teeth, something quite different begins to appear in human nature. The urge arises to learn from authority, to learn from those who already can do something. This urge lasts until the time of sexual maturity, until about fourteen or fifteen years of age. Thus, this natural drive fills the time in elementary school. We can properly teach in elementary school only if we have a thorough pedagogical understanding of this revolution within the child of seven. Here I have given you only a single example of what, compared to the old way, the new pedagogy must thoroughly observe and understand.

On the other hand, we need to know that around the age of nine new inner physical and spiritual strengths begin to come forth. If we were to teach prematurely what the curriculum foresees for the age after nine, the instruction, instead of helping, would damage the child for life.

We need a comprehensive understanding of human life if we want to practice a comprehensive, a true, pedagogy serving humanity. We must know how to teach before and after the children reach the age of nine. We may not, as old, gray-haired administrators from the school board do, set up the curriculum to take into account just any external consideration: this for the first grade; this for the second grade; this for the third grade; and so forth. Nothing that could really prepare the child for life will result. Human nature itself must teach us what we need to accomplish through education in each year of the child's life.

Consider for a moment that, as adults, you are still learning from life. Life is our great teacher. However, the ability to learn from life comes at the earliest at fifteen, sixteen or seventeen years of age. Then, we first stand face to face with the world in a way such that we can learn directly from the world. Until then, the teacher who faces us in the classroom is the world. It is the teacher we want to understand; it is the teacher we want to love; it is from the teacher we want to learn. The teacher should bring to us what is out there in the world. From the age of seven to fifteen years, there is an abyss between ourselves and the world. The teacher should bridge that gulf for us.

Can teachers who are not gripped by all that life has to give, who, embittered and soured by all that has been funneled into

them, "teach grammar so, natural history so, and other subjects so," who do not concern themselves with what so agi-
tates humanity in our time—can such teachers rightly depict
and reveal to children all that life brings over the seven or
eight years of elementary school? A new study of humanity, a
new understanding of humanity is necessary. The faculty
must develop a new enthusiasm out of this new understanding of humanity.

This shows you some of what we keep in mind in preparing for the children in our teaching seminars: to thoroughly
understand humanity so that we can teach from human
nature itself and send the child into life.

The second thing that we must develop as we work toward
a more humane form of society is a social attitude of the
teachers toward the children already in the school. This is a
new love of humanity—an awareness of the interplay of
forces between the teacher and pupil. Those forces cannot
exist if the teacher does not enter into the art of teaching in a
lively way.

Everyone agrees that the painter must learn to paint, that
the musician must have command over a musical instrument
and much more, that the architect must learn architecture.
We set certain requirements so these people may become artists. We also must set these kinds of requirements for teachers
who would become true human artists. We must set them
seriously. To do so, we must understand that no present-day
pedagogy and no present-day educational method gives the
teacher what must first be found through a thorough study of
humanity. We must find it so that a new love of humanity
may come into the relationship between teacher and pupil.
Our goal must be that teachers become true artists in their
field.

Many things play a role. One teacher enters the classroom,
and the children feel an aversion that lasts throughout the

year; they would much rather be outside because what that teacher does with them is so unpleasant. Another teacher need only enter the classroom and, simply by being present, creates a bridge to each pupil. What makes such a difference? The teacher who makes such an adverse impression on the children goes into the school only to, as the saying goes, earn a living—in order to live. That teacher has acquired the superficial ability to drill the children, but goes just as unwillingly to school as the children and is just as happy when school ends. That teacher does the job mechanically.

I am not surprised that the majority of today's teachers view their work mechanically. Their understanding of humanity comes from the dead science that has arisen out of the industrial, statist and capitalist life of the past three or four centuries. That science has resulted in a dead art of education, at best a wistful form of education. We are striving for the understanding of humanity that we need to create the art of teaching in the Waldorf school. This vision of humanity, this understanding of humanity, so penetrates the human being that of itself it generates enthusiasm, inspiration, love. Our aim is that the understanding of humanity that enters our heads should saturate our actions and feelings as well. Real science is not just the dead knowledge so often taught today, but a knowledge that fills a person with love for the subject of that knowledge.

Thus, this understanding of humanity is brought to the teachers, in the seminar they are now taking to prepare themselves to educate your children. This understanding of humanity, this understanding of the growing child, should so saturate the teachers that a love of humanity enters the teaching. As recompense for the love that the teachers provide the children, a power will come forth, will well up from the children, that gives them the ability to take in more easily the material to be learned. The right kind of love, not overly protective love, but

the real love that flows through what we do in the classroom or other teaching activities, determines whether the child will learn with ease or difficulty, whether the child's education is good or bad.

The third thing that we want to bring to the child and for which we prepare our teachers so that they understand the proper way to present it to the children, is willpower. We want to cultivate this willpower by allowing the child to do something artistic at a relatively early stage of childhood. Most people do not know the secret connection between the will and working in the proper way in childhood with drawing, painting, music and the other arts. We do so much good when the child has this opportunity.

Our children will learn to read and write from life itself. This is our intention. We will not pedantically force them to write letters that for every child at first seem all the same. They need not learn it as an abstract thing, as letters were for the North American Indians when the Europeans came. It is true, isn't it? The Europeans destroyed the North American Indians down to the root. One of the last chiefs of the North American Indian tribes destroyed by the Europeans tells that the white man, the paleface, came to put the dark man and all he stood for under the earth. "The dark man had certain advantages over the palefaces," the chief then continued; "he did not have the little devils on paper." We want to say that everything teachers pedantically and narrow-mindedly draw on the blackboard for the pupils to copy is seen as little devils by today's children. We can draw all such things from life. If we succeed in what we are attempting, the children will learn to read and write more quickly. When we derive everything from life, when writing comes from drawing and not from arbitrariness, children will learn more quickly. At the same time, we can raise strong-willed people who later in life will be up to the task.

We will not simply superficially say, "We want to educate people." In a profound manner, we first ask ourselves, modestly and honestly, "What is the Being of Humanity, and how does it appear in the developing Human Being?" We do not first go and ask political and industrial leaders, "How should we teach and educate people so that they can take their place in society?" We also do not ask, "What does this or that governmental body compel us to teach so that people can fulfill what the state demands of them?" No, we turn our questions to the uniform nature of humanity and its requirements. Yes, you see, in this respect the old social conditions are in conflict with what is necessary for a more socially oriented human future.

Today the state takes over the developing person, the child, at a particular age. The state would take over the child earlier, but the child is not clean enough for it. For a while, it leaves the rearing of and caring for the child to the parents. When the child has grown enough that it is no longer so dirty, the state takes over and dictates what we are to funnel into the child. Of course, the state allows us to funnel into the child only what is necessary for the workplace, thereby enabling itself to do with people as it will. Even when they are adults, people are often quite satisfied. The state tells them, "You will be assured of a lifelong job, and when you are no longer able to work, you will have a pension." Retirement is a notion that some circles of leading people treat as an ideal. They expect it from the state education. These people also expect that the state, through the religion teachers, will take their souls in hand so that these souls need not work, since the churches will do the work for them. They expect that the churches will, so to speak, provide a "soul retirement" after death. Today everyone wants to have everything done for them. This is the result of a totally false education.

Much must happen in the outside world to create better social conditions. Much must happen in just the area where the Waldorf school wants to set a foundation stone for this great building. It would be something beautiful for you to say with heartfelt meaning, "We want to be pioneers for a future educational system. We want to be pioneers in the sense that we want to be the first to entrust our children to such an educational system of the future, one working for a new social life. We want to be pioneers in the sense that we do not believe that a few external changes will lead to a better social condition, but that a change must occur at the heart of science, art and education to bring about the desired condition of humanity."A real education takes care that body, soul and spirit will be intrinsically free and independent. A real education takes care to put people into life. Do you believe that if we really ask people how we should bring them up, that is, if we inquire into the nature and being of humanity, we would then create impractical people? No, just the opposite! We are educating people who can, in truth, put themselves powerfully into life. In grammar school we are educating humans who, in later life, will know more of what is necessary for the outward, practical life. These people will have learned to think; these people will have learned to correctly feel; and these people will have learned to properly use their will. We want to introduce all of this, so that truth and strength can rule, not so that in pedagogy the phrase holds, "We should bring up children correctly." We should instead make the child a true person!

How do people today often imagine what should actually happen? Socialization should occur, but most people, even those who quite honestly speak of socialization, think, "Sure, somewhere there are the universities, and they have already done everything right. It may be that we need to change the outward position of the university professors a little, but science itself, we may not change that in any way." Middle school, high school, trade school—people just do not think that outward life has come from these schools. But the people educated in these schools have created the outer life. At most, we think we should organize the lower level of education somewhat differently than it is now. This results in self-deception, in that we say, "We must provide education without cost." I would like to know how we can, in fact, do this. We just deceive ourselves, since we must pay for education. It cannot be free of cost—that is only "possible" through the deception of taxes or such things. We make up such phrases, which do not have any basis in reality.

People think that we should change this or that in the organization a little. We must subject everything to fundamental change, from top to bottom. We need another teacher training, another spirit in the school, even another love, different from that which modern sophisticated faculties bring into the schools. Unfortunately, all too few people think about that. You will perform a great service to humanity if you are pioneers in this respect, if you think we must renew the educational system for the betterment of humanity, and if you take part in this renewal with heartfelt interest and heartfelt sense. The more you think of taking part, of interesting yourselves in what is to happen in the Waldorf School, the better the faculty will succeed in working in unity with you for the betterment and blessing of your children, and thus for the whole of future humanity—at least within the boundaries that we can envision now.

People can work out ideals alone and write them down. The ideals can be beautiful and can please this or that person. Yes, people can think abstract ideals alone. But, with ideals that we should put into practice, such as the ideal of our new educational system, we are dependent upon finding understanding in the world. We want especially the parents of the children to be entrusted to the Waldorf School to be understanding of its ideal.

...as spoken of his responsibility, and he is right.
...sibility, though, is something that goes much fur-
e are all conscious of this responsibility as we prepare
.ne Waldorf School, and we will always remain conscious
of it. Such a responsibility is always before us, when we work
toward an ideal as radical as that of the Waldorf School. By
taking up this ideal, we are forced to break with prejudices in
the broadest sense. Truly, today it is not easy to find out
everything we must do to educate children properly, particularly in grammar school. The empty phrase has caused such
great havoc.

"We should teach the children through play." This is particularly the ideal of middle-class mothers who, through a certain kind of love—we might call it a doting affection—are
devoted to their children. From one side we may emphasize,
with a certain right, that education should not become drudg-
ery for the child. We could take the position that we should
"playfully" carry out education. We are all quite clear that in
education we must bring play as well as work together in the
proper relationship to prepare for life. However, we are also
conscious that play which trains the child like an animal is play
no longer. This play, often found in our schools today, trains
the children like animals, just as before we pedantically drilled
them. Play can only occur in freedom. However, play must
alternate with another kind of activity so that children learn
the seriousness of work, so that they are up to the seriousness
of work in life. We will not work with empty phrases. We will
have a time for work and a time for play. We will judge everything by the manifestations of the nature of the developing
person, of the child.

Just as we should familiarize ourselves with the true understanding of humanity, so must we gradually bring the school
to the point that the children happily go to it, that they are
glad to go to this school. We will not seek to attain anything

unnatural. It would be unnatural to believe that children, who should have vacation, should go to school and not play during vacation. We will also not be so foolish as to believe that children, after they have played for weeks, should sit well-behaved in the classroom upon just returning to school. We will understand our children. However, after awhile, through the way that we relate to the children, they will do their work during school time just as happily as they play during vacation. An ideal of the Waldorf School is that the children do what they should do, out of an inner force. We do not see our goal as simply to command the children. Rather, our goal is to relate to the children so that from our attitude the children feel, "I am glad to do this, I am happy to go through this with my teacher."

When your children come home from school, we hope that you enjoy it when they talk about the things they enjoyed at school. We hope that you enjoy the joyous faces of the children when they come home after school. We do not hope this because we want to make life into some sort of entertainment, but because we know how many of today's terrible social conditions result from something that could be different. We know that worse will come to humanity if we do not work for new social circumstances through conscientious new beginnings in education. We do everything possible to form education and upbringing as I have described it to you, not to do the child a favor, but because we know the power that joy gives to the child.

We want to create this new school as an example—this school so many people hunger for, but do not have the courage to look in the eye. We will have to believe, we will have to understand, that the so-called social question also rests upon the problem of education as I characterized it here, and that we can accomplish social change only in the way that we are attempting in the Waldorf School. It would be a great tragedy if the social impulse that is the foundation of the Waldorf School were ignored. May it first be recognized by those who entrust their children to the Waldorf School. We are all conscious of the responsibility of placing something in the world to which you should entrust the development and future of your children, come what may. We have not taken on the responsibility of what should happen here out of some sort of whim, but out of the recognition that such tasks are necessary in our time and that it is now particularly necessary to come to the developing human being, the child, with the best that humanity can understand.

I do not know if you know exactly the feeling of having gone through the world during these terrible war years, the last four or five years, and having seen how the children, the six- to nine-year-olds or still younger, have grown up. At times, you could feel quite a deep pain if you did not live unconsciously and thoughtlessly in the world, but lived, rather, with a consciousness of what lies ahead if we do not conceive some help for what has brought humanity to such a terrible state. You get a heavy heart, seeing the growing children lately. You cannot see them without having a deep heartache, if you do not decide at the same time, as far as you are able, to effect another way of bringing up children—a way that is different from the way people of today had to go, the way that has caused so much of the present unhappiness and misery. In the foremost sense, we create a piece of human future with education. We must be clear that we must relearn, must rethink, many things. Today, we experience many curious things from teachers in the upper and lower grades.

I recently spoke in a neighboring city that has a university. I said that, among other things, the social question also involves the fact that people, although depressed by questions about the organization of life, do not consider themselves to be in an inhumane condition. I expanded upon that further.

Afterward—it is hard to believe that today such people still exist—a university professor came up and said he could not understand why an inhumane existence of the modern blue-collar worker was connected with the wage scale. He saw their situation as no different from that of, for instance, Caruso, who sings, and receives a payment of thirty to forty thousand marks for the evening. That would be just the same as when a blue-collar worker received his wages and as when he, as a professor, received his salary. He could see no difference. There would be only a difference in the size of the payment, but no essential difference. Therefore he could not see wages as being a degradation of human existence. Wages are wages.

That is the response we receive today from a highly educated teacher. We receive such responses also from teachers at lower schools. This only emphasizes the necessity for a renewal of our training and educational system. We can say, "Truly, today, when we hear what people around many higher schools say about a reformation of our social conditions, and about the necessity to reform the schools, that is the most vivid proof that we must reform these schools. These people can only say what they say because these schools have a form that we must change."

Now, two things could happen. Mr. Molt has had the ideal to found the school which today and over the next eight days shall be ceremoniously opened. Due to the peculiar circumstances of our time, people could misunderstand his intention. Resistance could arise so that we could not put this ideal into practice, and it would disintegrate after a short time. Then we would say, "Yes, Mr. Molt wanted something quite ideal, but it was utopian. No one can put something like that into practice so easily." Why is it utopian? It is utopian because it is not understood, or because it is resisted!

A second thing could happen. Understanding could arise for what is born out of true social understanding, understanding for the real practicality of this wish. Then what is desired will become customary. It will become so familiar, that at first you, and later others, will say, "There was someone who saw more practically than others who thought they knew all about practical life." People will not say, "This was utopian." People will say, "Something really practical was put into the world!"

May the second of these two possibilities come to pass! Those who have the heart and soul for the social development of humanity now and in the future see this as a necessity. We will be able to look with utmost satisfaction upon what will occur when you, the first to send your children to the Waldorf School, stand by the side of the teachers with understanding, with interest. That will be the beginning of what should thrive with this school, what can really prosper.

May it prosper! May it thrive, so that those who see this blossoming decide to do the same in many different places. Of course, only when, and may it be as soon as possible, the same takes place out of the same spirit in many places, only then can what should come out of the Waldorf School come out of it. Then soon many more will follow. The free spirit will rule and a free social training and educational system will spread over the civilized earth.

This spirit and this feeling will be instilled into the civilized earth and will be an important power for all that will help us to come to a better, more humane existence in social organization.

May we grasp that the social question is a manifold one, and that one of its most important aspects is the question of education. May understanding and vision arise in the hearts of many people and powers for thinking, feeling and willing arise in the children. Thus, these children, when they are grown, can look back thankfully to their parents, who stood and first saw the social question, but still suffered deprivation because they themselves could not be brought up within the new socially oriented education. To these parents who understand the idea of such an education, the children will look back thankfully. Those children will be carried into a new time, along with many others, by the power that has become theirs through a truly humane upbringing and a humane education.

People want to make children useful for life in many ways. The old teachers also said that. Through the new educational system and pedagogy, we want to put people more humanely into life. Through these children, raised in this way, life itself will be so formed that its humanness appeals to the decency of understanding people.

May this spirit rule in the founding of this work that Mr. Molt, through the Waldorf School, wants to give to a part of humanity.


## From the Question Session Following the Lecture

*Question*: How will religious instruction be given in the Waldorf School? Also, how will the feelings of the children coming from other schools be taken into account?

*Dr. Steiner*: It must first be emphasized that, in the strictest sense, the Waldorf School does not teach a particular philosophy. We are not going to bring dogmatically to the children what we derive from a philosophy that has been stated here for years. We will use it only because we can use it to improve, to reform the instructional methods, the way of handling the instruction.

On the other hand, we must, because our modern time needs it, present the content of the child's religion. A Catholic teacher will instruct Catholic children in the Catholic tradition; a Catholic teacher will lead them in their religious exercises.

The same is true for Protestant children. We do not seek to achieve the goals of the Waldorf School through the inculcation of any particular philosophy. What we want is that a new method of instructing and handling instruction, a new method of teaching and handling teaching arises out of what we do.

What happens to the children coming from other schools is a very important question, particularly for the older children. We will not begin with the first grade and then build upon that. Rather, we will begin with a complete elementary school. Thus, we will have children of all ages. Of course, through the methods we are now discussing in our seminar, we will later be able to do many things differently, when we have only children whom we taught beginning in the first grade. However, we will now take into account everything that the children have already learned. In each grade, we will begin with what the children have already learned and continue in the way appropriate to our methods. We will seek out only what is advantageous for the children without needing to repeat what they have already learned. In instructing, we can work very economically. Lay people have no idea of what we can accomplish. When we work so economically, we can teach in a quarter of an hour what normally takes two hours. This is a question of method; however, people must know the method. This is a very important thing, that we can teach in a quarter of an hour something that takes two hours to teach through incorrect methods. In that we use the right method, that is, a method that is in accord with human nature, we can teach more economically and accomplish much that other schools cannot accomplish, and still meet the criteria of the public school system. In this way, so long as we still have the present school system, when children graduate from our school, they can enter other schools without any loss of time. We will keep such things in mind.

# 2

# A Public Lecture
# on Waldorf Education

AARAU — NOVEMBER 11, 1921

WHEN, after the collapse of Germany in 1918, a movement toward social renewal was born in Stuttgart with the aim of lifting the country out of the chaos of the times and guiding it toward a more hopeful future, one of the oldest friends of the anthroposophical movement, Emil Molt, conceived the idea of founding the Waldorf school in Stuttgart. Mr. Molt was in a position to implement that idea almost immediately, for he was in charge of an industrial enterprise employing a large number of workers. Thanks to the excellent relations existing between the management of that enterprise, the Waldorf-Astoria Cigarette Factory, and its workers, it proved possible to attract all of the workers' children to the school. In this way, more than two years ago, the Waldorf school was founded, primarily for working class children.

During the past two years, however, the school has grown almost from month to month. Today we have not only the original pupils of the Waldorf school—whose guidance was put into my care—but also many other children from all social classes and backgrounds. Indeed, the number of pupils who have found their way into the Waldorf school from all quarters of the population is now considerably larger than the original number of founding pupils, the children of the factory workers.

This fact shows the Waldorf school to be in practice a school for children of all types, coming from different classes and cultures, all of whom receive the same teaching, based on our own methods.

The idea of the Waldorf school grew out of the anthroposophical movement, a movement that, nowadays, attracts a great deal of hostility because it is widely misunderstood. In tonight's talk, and by way of introduction, I will mention only one such misunderstanding. This misunderstanding asserts that it is the aim of anthroposophy or spiritual science, particularly in its social aspects, to be revolutionary or somehow subversive, which is not at all the case. I must emphasize this because it is of special importance for our pedagogical theme. As anthroposophical spiritual science seeks to deepen and fructify the many branches of science that have developed in the cultural and spiritual sphere during the last three or four centuries, it has no intention whatever of opposing modern science in any way. Nor does it wish to introduce amateurism into modern science. It only wishes to deepen and to widen the achievements of modern science, including modern medicine.

Likewise, the education arising from anthroposophical spiritual science does not wish to oppose the tenets of recent educational theory as put forward by its great representatives. Nor does it wish to encourage amateurism in this field either. Acknowledging the achievements of modern natural science, anthroposophical spiritual science has every reason to appreciate the aims and the achievements of the great educators at the end of the nineteenth and the beginning of the twentieth centuries. Anthroposophy has no wish to oppose them. It wishes only to deepen their work by what can be gained through anthroposophical research. It wishes to stand entirely on the ground of modern pedagogical thinking. However, it does find it necessary to expand the scope of modern pedagogical thinking and I shall endeavor to give a few outlines of how this is to be done.

Though the Waldorf school takes its starting point from anthroposophical spiritual science, it is nevertheless not an ideological school—and this I hope will be accepted as an important fact. The Waldorf school is not in the least concerned with carrying into the school anthroposophical dogma or anthroposophical convictions. It seeks to be neither ideological nor sectarian nor denominational, for this would not be in character with anthroposophical spiritual science. Unfortunately, the opposite is often erroneously believed.

The Waldorf school, which has its roots in anthroposophy, is a school applying specific methods and classroom practices, as well as pedagogical ideas and impulses drawn from anthroposophically-oriented spiritual science. When we founded the school, we were simply not in a position to insist on such radical demands as are frequently made by some modern educators who maintain, for instance, that, if one wants to educate children properly, one has to open boarding schools or the like in the country, away from cities. There are many such endeavors today, and we have no objection to them on our part. From their point of view, we fully understand the reasoning behind their demands. In the Waldorf school, however, we are not in the same happy position. We had to accept a given situation. The possibility was granted to us to place what was to become the Waldorf school in a city, in the very life of a city. There was no question of first insisting on the right outer conditions for the school. What mattered was to achieve what had to be achieved through the principles and methods of our education under given circumstances.

It is a characteristic feature of anthroposophical spiritual science that it can adapt itself to any outer conditions, for it wants to be able to work under all conditions of life. It has no wish to chase after utopian ideals, but wants to create something in harmony with the human potential of its members out of the immediate practical conditions and the practical needs of life in any given situation.

To repeat, no dogma is to be carried into the school. What a person standing within the anthroposophical movement does gain, however, is a way of knowing that involves our whole humanity. The educational life of our times tends to favor a certain intellectualism. Therefore there is no need to fear that the Waldorf school teaches its pupils that a human being consists not only of a physical body (as you can read in many anthroposophical writings) but also of an etheric body, supplying the formative and organic growing forces at work in the physical body, and also of an astral body that, during earthly life, carries what was developed during pre-earthly existence—prior to physical birth or, rather, conception, and so on—into the human physical organization. None of this is taught in the school. But, if we know that human beings, when observed with scientific accuracy, consist of body, soul, and spirit, and if we grasp how this is revealed in the child as a human being in the making, we gain a deeper and truer knowledge of the human being than is possible through present-day natural science.

We do not grasp this deeper knowledge of human beings and all that anthroposophical spiritual science can learn about them only with our powers of thinking: the whole human being— thinking, feeling, and willing—is involved. This, however, is not the substance from which the training methods for work in the Waldorf school are to be drawn. Rather, anthroposophical knowledge creates in our teachers the forces of will to do all that they can for growing children in accordance with the demands of each child's organization. However paradoxical it might sound, the child is the teacher "par excellence" in the Waldorf school. For Waldorf teachers are fully convinced that what they meet in their children, week by week, year by year, is the outer manifestation of divine and spiritual beings who have come down to earth from a purely soul and spiritual existence in order to evolve in a physical body on earth between birth and death. They realize that each child's being unites—by means of the stream of heredity coming through the parents and their ancestors— with what is bestowed physically and etherically. Waldorf teachers have an enormously deep reverence for the young human being who, in the first days after birth, already shows how an inner soul-being manifests in physiognomy, in the first limb movements, and in the first babblings that gradually grow into human speech. Anthroposophical knowledge of human beings creates a deep reverence for what the divine world has sent down to earth and that inner attitude of reverence is the characteristic feature of Waldorf teachers as they enter their classrooms every morning. From the daily revelations of this mysterious spirit and soul existence, they discover what they as teachers must do with their children.

This is the reason why one cannot formulate the methods of the Waldorf school in a few abstract rules. One cannot say: point one, point two, point three, and so on. Rather, one has to say that, through anthroposophical spiritual science, a teacher comes to know the growing human being and learns to observe what looks out of a child's eyes and reveals itself in a child's fidgety leg movements. Because teachers are thoroughly grounded in an understanding of the whole human being, their knowledge of anthroposophy fills not only their intellect, with its capacity to systematize, but embraces the whole human being who also feels and wills. These teachers approach their pupils in such a way that their methods acquire a living existence that they can always modify and metamorphose, even in larger classes, to suit each individual child.

Anyone hearing all of this in the abstract, might well respond, "These crazy anthroposophists! They believe that a human being does not only have a physical body which, as a corpse, may be carefully examined and investigated in physiology and biology; they also believe that human beings have etheric, and even astral, bodies; and they believe that we can know these if we practice certain soul exercises; they believe that if we strengthen our thinking to the point where the whole human being is transformed into a kind of 'supersensible sense organ'—if I may use Goethe's expression—we can see more than we do in ordinary human life." It is easy to poke fun at such "crazy anthroposophists," who speak in these terms of supersensible beings in the sense-perceptible world. But if these convictions—based not on weird fantasies but on well-grounded knowledge—are carried into teaching, those whose task it is to educate the young are able to look upon growing children realistically as beings of body, soul, and spirit. And this is how children must be observed if our pupils' innermost being is to be revealed.

I do not wish to say anything derogatory about what, today, is referred to as experimental psychology or experimental pedagogy. I appreciate what those scientific disciplines are capable of achieving and I acknowledge it. But, just because of those disciplines, we must deepen our educational life all the more. For, aside from their positive aspects, they demonstrate that we are not getting closer to children in a direct and natural way, but that, on the contrary, we have become more estranged from them than ever before. External experiments are made with children to ascertain how their thinking, their memory, and even their will function. From the ensuing statistics, rules and regulations are then drawn up. Certainly, such findings have their uses, especially if one is an anthroposophist. But, if we regard them as the "be-all and end-all" and a foundation for education, we only adduce proof that, in actual fact, we have not reached the child's real being in any way. Why do we find it necessary to engage in experiments at all? Only because the direct, immediate relationship of teacher to child, which was there in ancient, Biblical times—if I may use this expression—has been lost under the influence of our modern materialistic culture. External experiments are made because there no longer exists a direct feeling and understanding for what actually happens within a child. The fact of these external experiments is in itself proof that we have lost a direct relationship with our children and that we should try to rediscover it with all available power.

When we study contemporary experimental psychology and pedagogy, it often seems as if the experimentalist were like someone observing a person riding a horse to see how he or she does on a smooth path as compared to more difficult terrain. From such observations, the experimentalist then compiles statistics: on the smooth path, such and such a distance in fifteen minutes; on a slippery path, so many miles; on an uneven path, so many more miles; and so on. This is the way of working that we also find, more or less, in experiments made to determine whether a child will remember something for a quarter of an hour, or whether a child omits so and so many of the words to be remembered, and so on. To return to our simile; if we were to compile statistical details about the rider, we would have to take into consideration not only the state of the paths but also what the horse was capable of doing on the particular paths observed, and so on. But we will never succeed by this method in discovering anything about the rider him- or herself (although it would of course be perfectly possible to include the rider in statistical observations as well). What really matters is not just that we carry out external experiments on those to be educated, but that, as teachers, we are in direct, natural contact with children through our understanding of their inner nature.

In anthroposophical spiritual science, one learns to know what is given when a baby is born. We learn that a child bears within itself not only what we can perceive with our senses but also a spirit-soul being that has united with the physical embryo. We learn to know exactly how this spirit-soul being develops, just as we learn from material science how the physical germ develops within the hereditary flow. We learn to recognize that, independent of the inherited traits, something of a supersensible spirit and soul nature enters. Without teaching it as a dogma—and I must emphasize this repeatedly—this perspective nevertheless becomes a means of orientation for the teacher—something that serves to guide a teacher's observations of children even before they enter school.

In the case of a child learning to speak, the following premise is useful. We must observe not only what belongs to the stream of heredity but also what develops in the child from spiritual depths. Language is part of this. When one observes human beings in the light of anthroposophical spiritual science—discriminating between the more inward, astral body and the more outward etheric body—one comes to know the nature of the human will in quite a new way. One sees the will as more allied to the astral body while thinking, for instance, is seen to be more closely connected with the etheric body. One learns to know how these members interact in speaking. For in observing and experiencing life, we have to do not only with outer facts but with placing these facts in the right light.

Let us now take a well trained observer of life, someone schooled in anthroposophy to know human beings, and place this person beside a child who is going through the process of learning to speak. If we have really learned to look into a child's soul life, recognizing the imponderables at play between adult and child, we can learn more about children's psychology by observing real-life situations than, for example, the eminent psychologist Wilhelm Preyer[1] did by means of statistical records. For instance, we learn to recognize the immense difference between, let us say, when we hear a mother or father speaking to a child to calm it down and saying, "Ee Ee," and when we hear someone who is speaking to a child about something more outward in its immediate environment and says, "Hsh, hsh!" With every vowel sound, we speak directly to a child's feeling life. We address ourselves to the innermost being of the child's soul. With the help of spiritual science, we learn to know how to stimulate a particular soul area. And in this way, we bring about a certain connection between adult and child that generates a close relationship between teacher and pupil, allowing something to flow from the teacher directly to the child's inmost feeling.

If, for example, we speak to a child about how cold it is outside, that child is taken into the realm of consonants (as in "Hsh-Hsh"), where we work directly on the child's will. We can thus observe that we stimulate in one instance a child's feeling life, and in another the child's life of movement, which lives in will impulses.

With this example, I merely wanted to indicate how light can be shed upon everything, even the most elementary things, provided we have a comprehensive knowledge of life. Today, there exists a magnificent science of language from which education certainly can benefit a great deal. That science, however, studies language as if it were something quite separate from human beings. But, if we are schooled in anthroposophical spiritual science, we learn to look at language not as something floating above human beings who

---

1. Wilhelm Preyer, 1841–1897, physiologist and psychologist, published the book, *The Soul of the Child*, Leipzig, 1881.

then take hold of it and bring it into their lives; we learn that language is directly connected with the whole human being, and we learn to use this knowledge in practical life. We learn how a child's inner relationship to the vowel element is connected with a warming glow in the feeling life, whereas the consonantal element—whatever a child experiences through consonants—is closely linked to the movements of the will.

The point is that one learns to observe the child more intimately. This kind of observation, this empathy with the child, has gradually been lost. So often today, when attempts are made to educate young human beings, it is as if we were actually circumventing the child's real being—as if our modern science of education had lost direct contact with the child to be educated.

We no longer recognize that speech is organically linked to all processes of growth and to all that happens in a child. Fundamentally, we no longer know that, in raising a child to become an imitator in the right way, we are helping it become inwardly warm and rich in feelings. Until the change of teeth, around the seventh year, children depend entirely on imitation and all upbringing and education during those early years depends basically upon this faculty. Only if we gain a clear understanding of this faculty of imitation during the first years of life and can follow it closely from year to year will the hidden depths of a child's inner nature be revealed to us, so that we can educate our pupils in ways that, later on, will place them fully into life.

This is true not only of speech but of whatever we must teach our children before they enter school. As I say, until the second dentition, a child is, fundamentally speaking, wholly dependent on imitation. Anthroposophical spiritual science allows us to study the young child's faculty of imitation in all spheres of life—and speech, too, develops entirely through imitation. But the study of the faculty of imitation enables us to look more deeply into the nature of the growing human being in other ways too. Although contemporary psychology constantly thinks around the problem of how the human soul or—as it is sometimes called—the human spirit is connected to the human physical body, it is not in a position to come to any exact idea of the relationship between the human soul and spirit on one side and the physical and bodily counterpart on the other. Basically, psychology only knows the physical aspects of the human being, when, like a corpse, the body is bereft of soul and spirit; on the other hand, it has distanced itself from the human soul and spirit as I have spoken of them. This situation can best be clarified with the help of a particular example. Contemporary science does not appreciate the importance of such phenomena as the second dentition occurring around the seventh year. But the kind of observation fostered by spiritual science reveals how a child's soul forces change during this process. A child's memory and ability to think, and also a child's faculty of feeling, become very different during these years. Actually, one cannot see a child's soul life develop before about the seventh year. But where was this emerging soul life with which we have to deal when the child enters school before the seventh year? Where was it previously?

If, from an anthroposophical point of view, we study how a child's memory and will assume a particular configuration in the seventh year, we will not conclude that these new faculties have suddenly "flown into the child." We will assume that they developed within the child itself. But where were they previously? They were active in the child's physical organism. In other words, what the teacher must educate was previously a latent, hidden force in the child's own being. That force has been liberated. As long as children need the forces that will culminate with the pushing out of the second teeth, those forces will be active in the child's inner realm. With the shedding of the milk teeth and the emergence of the second teeth, those forces—like the latent heat in certain substances—are released from their task and reveal themselves as new soul and spiritual capacities. These we then actively engage in our teaching. The method employed by scientific thinking is perfectly appropriate in the inorganic realm. When physicists today study certain substances that emit heat after undergoing a particular process, they ascribe that heat to the warmth that was formerly contained within the substance as "latent" or hidden heat. Then they study how, when subjected to a particular process, that latent heat is liberated or released from the physical substance. They would not dream of concluding that the radiating heat had somehow come into the matter from outside, but they study the condition in which the heat existed while already present there. This way of thinking, inaugurated by physics, can be transferred to the more complicated realm of the human being.

Only by studying examples from real life can we learn to understand how soul and body work together. We can engage in endless philosophical speculation about the relationship of soul and body to each other but, when studying early childhood up to the seventh year, we must observe the actual facts. Only then will we recognize that forces that have left the organic bodily realm after the change of teeth are free to be used by the teacher in quite a new way.

The same principle applies to the whole span of human life. All of the speculative theories about the relationship of soul and body that we find in books on philosophy and physiology are useless unless they are based on a mode of observation that is exact according to proper scientific methods.

If we observe such things further, we realize that the forces in a child with which we deal as teachers are the same that were previously engaged in building up the organism. We know, too, that those forces must now assume another form and that, if we are to teach children, we must come to know those forces in their new form. But we must also get to know them in their original form—since they must be used for learning, we must be able to recognize them in their original task. Well, a lot more could be said about this. I will only point out that it is because of those forces, working in the depths of the organism, creating life, that a child imitates up to the seventh year. To understand a preschool child, we must always bear in mind this faculty of imitation.

For example, parents complain that their son has stolen money. They are looking for advice. You ask how old the child is and are told that he is four or five years old. It might sound surprising, but a child of four or five does not really steal. Such a child is still at the stage of imitation. And so, if you ask further questions, you discover, for instance, that the child has seen his mother taking money out of a cupboard every day. The child imitates this action and, consequently, he too takes money. I have even known a case in which a child took money out of a cupboard but, instead of buying sweets, bought things to give to other children. There was nothing immoral in this behavior, only perhaps something somewhat amoral, something imitative.

An incident like this makes us realize that, in educating children, we are dealing with imponderables. As teachers, we must realize that, when we stand before a child who is an imitator, we must be mindful even of our thoughts. Not only our actions but our thoughts too must be of a kind that a child can safely imitate. The entire upbringing of preschool children must be based on this principle of imitation. Even if it might sound strange, awareness of this principle must lie at the foundation of a really healthy form of early education.

The forces that make a child an imitator to such an extent that it imitates even the slightest hand movement appear when the child is about seven as the liberated forces with

which educators and teachers have to deal. Looking more closely at this development, one recognizes that, whereas a child is a compulsive imitator up to the age of seven, during the next seven years, up to puberty, the pupil needs to experience a natural sense of authority in the teacher as the right guide on life's path. The experience of authority becomes the main educational principle for children between the change of teeth and puberty—a principle that develops naturally to become the basic relationship between teacher and pupil.

It is all too easy to speak abstractly about this relationship based upon a natural sense of authority. If we wish to guide it in the right direction at every moment of our teaching life, we need anthroposophical knowledge of the human being.

Today, many people speak about the necessity and the importance of visual instruction, practical demonstration, and so forth—and they are in a certain sense quite right to do so. It is certainly right for some subjects. Anything that can be outwardly observed can be brought to the child by these methods. But we must consider, above all, the moral order of the world and human religious feelings—that is, everything pertaining to the spiritual nature of the world. The spiritual is imperceptible to outer senses and if we take the so-called visual instruction method too far, we lead children into believing in only what is sense perceptible—that is, into materialism. What really matters at this age is that through the natural relationship to the teacher, the child feels, "This adult, who is my guide, knows what is right and behaves in a way I long to emulate." (If I describe such a feeling as an adult, it is naturally quite different from how a child would experience it.)

During the first seven years, then, a child's activities mirror and imitate its surroundings—above all through gestures, including the subtle inner gestures that live in speech. But, in the next seven years, children develop under the influence of the words that come from the naturally accepted authority of their teacher. In order to appreciate the importance and value of this natural sense of authority, one must have a thorough foundation in true knowledge of the human being.

You would hardly expect someone like myself who, many years ago, wrote a book called *Intuitive Thinking as a Spiritual Path: A Philosophy of Freedom* to support a reactionary social belief in authority. So it is not on the basis of any authoritarian intention but solely on educational grounds that I maintain that the most essential principle, the most important force in education, between the age of seven and puberty, lies in a pupil's belief that the teacher, as an authority, knows what is right and does what is right. This must sink down into the child.

If students do not develop on the basis of this belief in the authority of the teacher, they will be unable, when older, to enter social life in a wholesome manner.

To understand this, we need only to know what it means for a child willingly to accept something on the basis of authority. I realize that this is for many people rather a controversial point but, actually, it is controversial only for those who, fundamentally speaking, lack the will to look at life in its entirety.

For instance, let us assume, say, that, in our second year of life nature did not dispose the form of our fingers so that they grow and develop—that nature made our fingers such that, as it were, they were cast in hard stereotyped forms. What would we do then! Insofar as we are human, then, we are growing, continuously changing beings. And as educators, likewise, this is the kind of essence that we must pour into children's souls. We must not impose on our children anything that creates sharply contoured pictures, impressions, or will impulses in them. Just as our fingers do not retain the contours that they had when we were two but rather grow on their own, so all ideas, thoughts, and feelings that we pour into children during their school years must have the essence of growth in them.

We must be quite clear: what we bring to an eight-year-old cannot be clear-cut or sharply contoured. Rather, it must have an inner capacity for growth. By the time the person is forty, it will have become something quite different. We must be able to see the *whole* human being. Anyone who does not appreciate the principle of authority during these years of childhood has never experienced what it really means when, for instance, in the course of one's thirty-fifth year, out of the dark recesses of memory, one understands some concept of history or geography—or some concept of life—that one accepted without understanding at the age of nine on the authority of a well loved teacher or parent, having taken it simply on faith. When such a concept emerges in the soul and is understood with the mature understanding of several decades later, this becomes an animating principle that calls up an indefinable feeling that need not be brought to full consciousness: something from one's earliest years lives on in one's soul. It is in this sense that we must be able to follow the forces of growth in nature.

Our educational principles and methods must not be tied up in fixed formulae. Rather, they must become a kind of refined, practical instinct for action in those who educate from a living knowledge of human beings. Teachers will then find the right way of dealing with children rather than merely artificially grafting something onto the souls in their care. This is not to deny what has been promulgated by the great pedagogues of the nineteenth and early twentieth centuries. On the contrary, it is actually applying it in the right way.

Those who wish to become Waldorf teachers know quite well that they cannot join the school as amateurs, as dilet-tantes. They must be moved by all that nineteenth- and twen-tieth-century education has brought forth. But, at the same time, they must also bring to the Waldorf school the living insight into human beings of which I have spoken. Here one feels prompted to quote Goethe's dictum, "Consider well the *what*, but consider more the *how*." You will find excellent expositions of the *what*—with regard to foundations and principles—in theoretical texts on education. Even quite idealistic thoughts are sometimes expressed there, but all of this represents only the *what*. The point is not to formulate abstract principles but to be able to apply them in a living way, with inner soul warmth.

I am fully convinced that if a group of people were to sit together—they need not even be outstandingly clever—to draft the blueprint for an ideal school, their schemes, put into order of priorities—first, second, third, and so forth—would be quite excellent. They would be so convincing that one could not improve on them. It is quite possible to think out the grandest ideals and turn them into slogans for great movements of reform and so on. But, in life as it is, all of this is of little value. What matters is to truly observe life, to bear in mind the living human being who is capable of doing what needs to be done under given circumstances. "Consider well the *what*, but consider more the *how*."

And so, what matters is that love of the child lies at the root of all of our educational endeavors, and that all teaching be done out of an inner, living experience. Against this background, the foundations of our education become quite other than they usually are. With this in mind, then, I would like to put into words a fundamental underlying principle, once more in the form of an example.

A child is supposed to form an inner picture of a definite concept. It is capable of doing so but, in our attempts to communicate something abstract—something of an ethical and religious nature—we can proceed in different ways. For example, let us imagine that the teacher wants to convey to pupils—naturally in accordance with the children's age and maturity—the idea of the immortality of the human soul. We can do this with a comparison. There are two ways in which we can do this. One would be as follows. As teachers, we can believe that we are terribly clever, whereas the child is still young and terribly ignorant. On this basis, we could invent a comparison and say, "Look at the chrysalis. The butterfly comes out of the chrysalis." Then, after describing this process pictorially, we might say, "Just as the butterfly emerges from its chrysalis, so the human soul, when a person passes through the portal of death, leaves the body and flies into the spiritual world." This is one way of approaching the problem. Feeling greatly superior to the child, we think out a simile or comparison. But, if this is our underlying attitude, we will not be very successful. Indeed, this is a situation where imponderables play their part. For a teacher who has been schooled in anthroposophical spiritual science about the nature of the world and knows that there is spirit in all matter will not proceed from a feeling of being far more clever than the child. Consequently, he or she will not invent something for the child's benefit. That is to say in this case the teacher will firmly believe that what on a higher level represents the human soul leaving the body at death is represented in the natural order on a lower level by the emergence of the butterfly from the chrysalis. The teacher will believe in the truth of this picture. To this teacher, the image is a sacred revelation. These are two entirely different approaches. If I speak to the child out of a sacred conviction, I touch the child's innermost being in an imponderable way. I call forth in the child a living feeling, a living concept. This approach is generally true. We must neither underestimate nor overestimate what modern science has to say out of its exclusive interest in the external world.

Allow me to quote a somewhat far-fetched example to consolidate what I have been saying. As you know, there has been a great deal of talk about so-called "counting horses." Those horses perform quite special feats. I myself have not seen the *Elberfeld* horses, but I did see Herr von Osten's horse and witnessed how this horse, when questioned, stamped out the answers to simple arithmetical questions with one of its hooves. The horse stamped the correct number of times— one, two, three, four, five, six, and so on. In order to explain such a phenomenon and avoid falling into nebulous mysticism or mere rationalism, we need a certain ability to observe. Now, among the spectators of the counting horses was a certain private tutor in psychology and physiology who, having seen Herr von Osten's horse performing its tricks, declared that the horse stamped when a specific number was called out because it was able to detect very subtle and refined expressions in Herr von Osten's face. He claimed that when his master moved his face in a certain way after asking, "What are three times three?" the horse stopped stamping after nine stamps. Naturally, this learned gentleman had to prove that such looks or movements really existed in Herr von Osten's face. But this he was unable to do. In his learned dissertation, he stated, "These looks are so subtle and infinitesimal that a human being cannot detect them, and even I myself"— he added— "am unable to say anything about them." You see that all of his cleverness amounted to admitting his own lack of being able to discover the facial expressions that the horse was supposed to follow. In other words, the horse was more perceptive than this learned lecturer! A less biased spectator would have noticed that, while the horse stamped answers to arithmetical questions, Herr von Osten continually fed his horse with sugar lumps which he took from his rather capacious coat pocket. While apparently performing calculations, the horse was constantly relishing the sweet taste of the sugar lumps. I must ask you not to misunderstand me if I say that this way of treating the horse gave rise to a very specific form of a loving and intimate relationship, an inner relationship, and that this is really what was the root cause of what was happening.

If one wants to discover this true relationship existing below the level of ordinary observation, one must begin with what the effect of such "love" can be. If one wants to understand such things properly, it is no good talking of hypnotism or suggestion in a general way, but one must understand the nature of such a subtle relationship. Neither nebulous mysticism nor mere rationalism will lead to one's solving the mystery, but only a knowledge of the human, and in this case also the animal, soul.

This is what matters above all if we wish to found a living method of education, as distinct from one based on mere principles and intellectual theories. This living method of education then guides us to observe the child from year to year. It is this *How*, this individual treatment of each child even within a larger class, that matters. It is possible to achieve it. The Waldorf school has already demonstrated this fact during the first few years of its existence.

Here I can only give broad outlines, which can be supplemented by more detailed examples. First of all, we receive the child into our first grade, where it is supposed to learn writing and reading, perhaps also the beginnings of arithmetic and so on. Let us first discuss reading. Reading in our present culture is really quite alien to a young child. If we go back to ancient times, we find that a kind of picture writing existed in which each letter word still retained a pictorial connection with the object it represented. In our present system of writing or printing, there is nothing to link the child's soul to what is written. For this reason, we should not begin by immediately teaching children writing when they enter primary school in their sixth or seventh year. In the Waldorf school, all teaching—and this includes writing, which we introduce before reading—appeals directly to a child's innate artistic sense. Right from the start, we give our young pupils the opportunity of working artistically with colors, not only with dry crayons but also with watercolors. In this simple way, we give the child something from which the forms of the letters can be developed. Such things have been done elsewhere, of course. But it is again a matter of *how*. The main thing is that we allow the child to be active without in any way engaging the forces of the intellect but by primarily activating the will. On the basis of drawing and painting, we gradually lead a child's first will activities in writing toward a more intellectual understanding of what is written. We lead our children, step by step, developing everything in harmony with their own inherent natures. Even down to the arrangement of the curriculum, everything that we do at school must be adapted to the child's evolving nature. But, for this, anthroposophical knowledge of human beings is necessary.

I would here like to point out how one can observe the harm done to children when one does not give them concepts and feelings capable of growth, but makes them aware of the difference between the outer material world of fixed forms and their own inner mobile soul life at too early an age. Until about the ninth year, a child does not yet clearly discriminate between him- or herself and the outer world. One must be careful not to believe in abstract concepts, as some people do today who say, "Well, of course, if a young child bumps into the corner of a table, it smacks the table because it thinks that the table is also a living thing." This, of course, is nonsense. The child does not think that the table is a living object. It treats the table as if it were a child, too, simply because it cannot yet distinguish its own self from the table. Whether the table lives or not is beside the point. The child, as yet, has no such concept. We must always deal with realities, not with what we ourselves imagine intellectually. Until the ninth year, whatever we introduce to a child must be treated as if it had purely human qualities. It must be based on the assumption that the children's relationship to the world is such that every thing is a part of them—as if it were a part of their own organism. One can, of course, point to certain obvious examples where a child will differentiate between something in the external world and its own being. But, between the seventh and ninth years, we cannot further the finer aspects of education unless we bring to life whatever we teach the child, unless we make everything into a parable, not in a dead, but a truly living form. Everything must be taught in mobile and colorful pictures, not in dead static concepts.

After this special moment in the ninth-tenth year, while all subjects had previously to be "humanized," teachers can begin to introduce simple descriptions of plants and animals in a more objective style. Then, between the eleventh and twelfth years, they can begin to introduce inorganic subjects, such as the study of minerals and physics. Certainly the lifeless world should be approached only after children have been fully immersed in the living world. Between the ninth and tenth years, a most important, significant moment occurs: it is only then that children really become conscious of the difference between their inner selves and their surroundings. This is the age when we can first intellectually introduce children to the life of plants and animals, both of whom have an existence apart from human beings. Something truly profound is taking place in a child's mind and soul at this time—a little earlier in the case of some children, a little later in others. Something is happening—fundamental changes are occurring—in the depths of their young souls; namely, they are learning to distinguish their inner selves from the outer world in a feeling way, but not yet by means of concepts. Therefore if teachers are aware of the right moment, and can find the appropriate words, they can—acting as the situation demands—do something of lasting value and importance for the whole life of these children aged between nine and ten. On the other hand, if they miss this significant moment, they can create an inner barrenness of soul or spiritual aridity in later life, and an attitude of everlasting doubt and inner dissatisfaction. But, if teachers are sufficiently alert to catch such a significant moment and if, by immersing themselves in the child's being, they have the necessary empathy and know how to speak the right words and how to conduct themselves rightly, they can perform an immense service for their children, who will derive benefit for the rest of their lives. In Waldorf education, the observation of such key moments in the lives of children is considered to be of utmost importance.

Thus the child is led—I mention only a few characteristic examples—to the age when school normally comes to an end, to the age of puberty.[2]

How many countless discussions and arguments are going on these days about puberty from a psychoanalytical and from a psychological point of view! The main thing is to recognize that one is dealing here with the end of a characteristic life period—just as second dentition represented the end of an earlier period of development. Puberty in itself is only a link in an entire chain of metamorphoses embracing the whole of human life. What happened in the child at second dentition is that inner soul forces became liberated that had previously been working within the organism. Between the seventh and approximately fourteenth years, we try to guide the child in the ways I just described. With the onset of puberty, however, children enter the time of life when they can form their own judgments on matters concerning the world at large. Whereas, when younger, our children drew their inner being from the depths of their organism, as adolescents they now become capable of understanding the spiritual nature of the outer

---

2. In 1921, the school-leaving age in Germany was fourteen.

world as such. How to educate our children between their seventh and fourteenth years so that they are naturally guided to acquire an independent and individual relationship to the world—of which sexual life is only one expression—presents one of the greatest challenges to teachers. This is one of the most important problems of a truly living education. The sexual love of one person for another is only one aspect, one part of the whole fabric of human social life.

We must lead our adolescents to the point where they develop the inner maturity necessary to follow outer events in the world with caring interest. Otherwise, they will pass them by unheeded. As teachers, we must aim at turning our young human beings into social beings by the time of puberty. We must also try to cultivate in them religious feelings, not in a bigoted or sectarian way, but in the sense that they acquire the seriousness necessary to recognize that the physical world is everywhere permeated by spirit. They should not feel inwardly satisfied with merely observing the outer sense world but should be able to perceive the spiritual foundations of the world everywhere.

During prepubescence, when pupils open their inner being to us, believing in our authority, we must be what amounts to the whole world for them. If they find a world in us as their teachers, then they receive the right preparation to become reverent, social people in the world. We release them from our authority, which gave them a world, into the wide world itself.

Here, in only a few words, I touch on one of the most important problems of cognition. If we train children to make their own judgments too early, we expose them to forces of death instead of giving them forces of life. Only teachers whose natural authority awakens the belief that what they say and do is the right thing, and who in the eyes of the child become representatives of the world, will prepare their pupils to grow into really living human beings when,

later on, they enter life. Such teachers prepare their pupils
not by controlling their intellect or their capacity to form
judgments but by setting the right example as living human
beings. Life can evolve only with life. We make our students
into proper citizens of the world by presenting the world to
them in a human being—the teacher—not through abstract
intellectual concepts.

I can characterize all of this in a few sentences, but what I
am suggesting presupposes an ability to follow in detail how
growing children evolve from day to day. By the power of his
or her example, the way in which a teacher carries something
through the door into the classroom already helps a child to
develop further toward finding its own way in life. If we know
this, we need not make amateurish statements, such as that all
learning should be fun. Many people say this today. Try to see
how far you get with such an abstract principle! In many
respects learning cannot bring only joy to the child. The right
way is to educate children by bringing enough life into the various subjects that they retain a curiosity for knowledge, even if
it does not reward them immediately with pleasure. How a
teacher proceeds should be a preparation for what pupils must
learn from them.

This leads quite naturally to cultivation of the pupils' sense
of duty. We touch here upon a sphere that extends far beyond
what belongs to the field of education. We touch on something where a method and practice of education based on spiritual foundations directly fructifies the whole of cultural life.

We all of us surely look up to Schiller and Goethe as leading spirits. To have studied and written about them for more
than forty years, as I have, leaves one in no doubt as to one's
full, warm appreciation of their work and gifts. There is, however, just one point that I would like to make in this context.

When, in the 1790s, Schiller, having distanced himself from
Goethe for all kinds of personal reasons renewed an intimate

friendship with him, he wrote his famous—and sadly too little appreciated—*Letters on the Aesthetic Education of Man*. Schiller wrote these letters under the influence of how Goethe worked, thought, and viewed the world. In those letters, which are about aesthetic education, we find a strange sentence: "Only when we play are we fully human, and we play only when we are human in the truest sense of the word." With that sentence, Schiller wanted to point out how ordinary life essentially chains us into a kind of slavery, how the average person, forced to live under the yoke of necessity, suffers under the burden of outer life. In general, people are free to follow their own impulses only when engaged in artistic activities, when creating and enjoying art, or when behaving like children at play, acting only in accordance with their own impulses. What Schiller describes in his aesthetic letters is a beautiful and genuine conception of what it is to be human.

On the other hand, the letters show that with the advance of our modern scientific, technological civilization and for the sake of human dignity, exceptional persons like Schiller and Goethe found it necessary to demand that human beings should be allowed freedom from the daily round of duties. To become fully human, people should be relieved of the coercion of work so that they can be free to play. If we bear in mind the social conditions imposed on us by the twentieth century, we realize that we have completely changed our attitude toward life. Realizing that everyone must accept the demands of life, we feel that we carry an intolerable burden of responsibility upon our shoulders.

We must learn how to make life worthwhile again, from both the social and individual points of view, not only by introducing more play but by taking up our tasks in a more human way. This is the reason why the social question is today first of all a question of education. We must teach young people to work in the right way. The concept of duty must be brought into school, not by preaching, but in the right and natural way—which can be achieved only through a thorough, well grounded, and correct knowledge of human nature.

If we do so, we shall be founding schools for work, not schools following the attitude that teaching and learning are merely be a kind of "playing about." In our school, where authority plays its proper part, pupils are expected not to shy away from the most demanding tasks. In Waldorf schools, students are encouraged to tackle whole heartedly whatever is to be mastered. They are not to be allowed to do whatever they feel like doing.

It is with this in view that the Waldorf school has been founded. Children are to learn to work in the right way; they are to be introduced to life in the world in the full human sense. This demands work for social reasons and also that, as human beings, the students should learn to face one another and, above all, themselves in the right way. For this reason, apart from conventional gymnastics, which originally evolved from human physiology and hence has its values, we have also introduced eurythmy[3]—a new art of movement, cultivating body, soul and spirit; a visible form of language and music—into the Waldorf school.

You can find out more about eurythmy in Dornach. Just as there are speech and music that you can hear, so there also is a kind of language and music that uses the medium of gestures and movements evolved from the organization of the human body, but not as is done in dance or mime. It can be performed by groups of people who express in this new way the kind of content that is usually expressed through audible speech and

3. See, for instance, Rudolf Steiner, *An Introduction to Eurythmy* (Hudson, New York: Anthroposophic Press, 1984) and Marjorie Spock, *Eurythmy* (Spring Valley, New York: Anthroposophic Press, 1980).

music. Since its introduction in the Waldorf school some two years ago, we have already been able to observe that pupils from the lowest to the highest grades take to eurythmy lessons with the same natural ease with which little children take to speaking, provided that the lessons are given properly, in a way suited to each age group.

Once, during an introductory talk before a eurythmy performance in Dornach, I spoke about eurythmy to an audience that happened to include one of the most famous physiologists of our times (you would be surprised if you heard his name). After saying that we had no wish to denigrate the value of gym in schools, but that the time would come when such matters would be judged with less prejudice and that eurythmy, with its movements involving a person's soul and spirit, would then come into its own, the famous physiologist approached me and said, "You said that gymnastics has its own beneficial value in modern education and that it is based on human physiology. As a physiologist, I consider gymnastics to be sheer barbarism!" It was not I who expressed this view, it was one of the best-known physiologists of our times!

Such an incident can lead us to appreciate the saying: "Consider well the *what*, but consider more the *how*." There are occasions when, reading books on educational theory and applied teaching, one feels like shouting for joy. *What* the great educationalists have achieved! But what matters is the right *how*. One has to find ways and means of implementing the ideas into practical life in the right way.

Every Waldorf teacher must seek this anew each day, for anything that is alive must be founded on life. Spiritual science eventually leads each one of us to an understanding of fundamental truths that, although they are always the same, nevertheless inspire us ever anew. Regarding our ordinary knowledge based on material things, we depend on our memory. What has been absorbed is remembered, to be recalled later from the store of memory. What we have once learned, we possess; it is closely linked to us. In everyday life, we certainly need our store of memory. Our intellect depends on memory, but living processes do not need memory—not even on the lower levels of our existence. Just imagine for a moment that you thought that what you ate once as a small child sufficed for the rest of your life. You have to eat anew every day because eating is a part of a living process and what has been taken up by the organism must be thoroughly digested and transformed. Spiritual substance likewise must be taken up in a living way and an educational method based on anthroposophy must work out of this living process.

This is what I wanted to describe to you in brief outline, merely indicating here what has been described in further detail in anthroposophical books, particularly those dealing with education. I wanted to draw your attention to the educational principles of the Waldorf school, a pioneering school founded by our friend Emil Molt, a school that has no desire to rebel against contemporary education. It seeks only to put into practice what has often been suggested theoretically. Anyone who surveys the kind of life which humanity, particularly in Europe, lives today will recognize the need to deepen many aspects of life. During the second decade of this twentieth century, following the terrible catastrophe that destroyed most of what was best in humanity, one must admit the importance of giving the coming generations soul-spiritual and physical-bodily qualities different from those received by our contemporaries who have had to pay so dearly in human life. Those who, as parents, must care for the well-being of their sons and daughters and who, most of all, have the right to see how education relates to life, will view our efforts without prejudice. Those among them who, as parents, have experienced the great catastrophes of our times, will doubtlessly welcome every attempt that, based on deeper social and spiritual awareness, promises the coming generations something better than what has been offered to many at the present time. The people who have most reason to hope for an improvement of conditions prevailing in contemporary education are the parents and they, above all, have the right to expect and demand something better from the teachers. This was the thinking and the ideal that inspired us when we tried to lay the educational foundations of the Waldorf school.

## From the Discussion

*Questioner:* Dr. Steiner has spoken to us about the importance of authority in education, but this is something with which our young people want nothing to do. Every teacher, not to mention every priest, experiences it. Various currents run through our younger generation and one can certainly notice an aloofness on their part toward anything connected with the question of authority, be the authority in the parental home or authority regarding spiritual matters. Parents sometimes have the feeling that they no longer have any say in anything and that one must simply let these young people go their own way. On the other hand, one sometimes also witnesses the disillusionment of such an attitude and it is then painful to see young people not finding what they were seeking. There is something in the air that simply seems to forbid a respectful attitude toward older people, something that is like a deep-seated sting, ever ready to strike against authority in whatever form. Perhaps Dr. Steiner would be kind enough to tell us something about the reasons for this strange ferment among the younger generation. Why are they not happy? Why do they take special pleasure in complaining? It saddens us that we are no longer able to reach them. I have sought help by studying books dealing with this problem, but I have so far not found a single one that could show me the way forward. I would therefore be very happy if Dr. Steiner could say something to give us insight into the soul of a young person.

*Rudolf Steiner:* This is, of course, a subject that, unfortunately, were I were to deal with it in any depth, would require a whole lecture of at least the same length as the one I have just given you—I say unfortunately because you would have to listen to me for such a long time! I would, however, like to say at least a few words in response to the previous speaker's remarks.

During my life, which by now can no longer be described as short, I have tried to follow up various life situations related to this question. On one hand, I have really experienced what it means to hear, in one's childhood, a great deal of talk about a highly esteemed and respected relative whom one had not yet met in person. I have known what it is to become thoroughly familiar with the reverence toward such a person that is shared by all members of the household, by one's parents as well as by others connected with one's upbringing. I have experienced what it means to be led for the first time to the room of such a person, to hold the door handle in my hand, feeling full of awe and reverence. To have undergone such an experience is of lasting importance for the whole of one's life. There can be no genuine feeling for freedom, consistent with human dignity, that does not have its roots in the experience of reverence and veneration such as one can feel deeply in one's childhood days.

On the other hand, I have also witnessed something rather different. In Berlin, I made the acquaintance of a well-known woman socialist, who often made public speeches. One day I read, in an otherwise quite respectable newspaper, an article of hers entitled, "The Revolution of our Children." In it, in true socialist style, she developed the theme of how, after the older generation had fought—or at least talked about—the revolution, it was now the children's turn to act. It was not even clear whether children of preschool age were to be included in that revolution. This is a different example of how the question of authority has been dealt with during the last decades.

As a third example, I would like to quote a proposal, made in all seriousness by an educationalist who recommended that a special book be kept at school in which at the end of each week—it may have been at the end of each month—the pupils were to enter what they thought about their teachers. The idea behind this proposal was to prepare them for a time in the near future when teachers would no longer give report "marks" to their pupils but pupils would give grades to their teachers.

None of these examples can be judged rightly unless they are seen against the background of life as a whole. This will perhaps appear paradoxical to you, but I do believe that this whole question can be answered only within a wider context. As a consequence of our otherwise magnificent scientific and technical culture—which, in keeping with its own character, is bound to foster the intellect—the human soul has gradually become less and less permeated by living spirit. Today, when people imagine what the spirit is like, they usually reach only concepts and ideas about it. Those are only mental images of something vaguely spiritual. This, at any rate, is how the most influential philosophers of our time speak about the spiritual worlds as they elaborate their conceptual theories of education. This "conceptuality" is, of course, the very thing that anthroposophical spiritual science seeks to overcome. Spiritual science does not want its adherents merely to talk about the spirit or to bring it down into concepts and ideas; it wants human beings to imbue themselves with living spirit. If this actually happens to people, they very soon begin to realize that we have gradually lost touch with the living spirit. They recognize that it is essential that we find our way back to the living spirit. So-called intellectually enlightened people in particular have lost the inner experience of living spirit. At best, they turn into agnostics, who maintain that natural science can reach only a certain level of knowledge and that that level represents the ultimate limit of what can in fact be known. The fact that the real struggle for knowledge only begins at this point, and that it leads to a living experience of the spiritual world—of this, generally speaking, our educated society has very little awareness.

Natural science is protected from falling into such clichés simply because of its close ties to experimentation and observation. When making experiments, one is dealing with actual spiritual facts that have their place in the general ordering of natural laws. But, excepting science, we have been gradually sliding into a life heavily influenced by clichés and phrases, by-products of the overspecialization of the scientific, technological development of our times. Apart from many other unhappy circumstances of our age, it is to living in such a phrase-ridden, clichéd language that we must attribute the problem raised by the previous speaker. For a child's relationship to an adult is an altogether imponderable one. The phrase might well flourish in adult conversations, and particularly so in party-political meetings, but if one speaks to children in mere phrases, clichés, they cannot make anything of them. And what happens when we speak in clichés—no matter whether the subject is religious, scientific, or unconventionally open-minded? The child's soul does not receive the necessary sustenance, for empty phrases cannot offer proper nourishment to the soul. This, in turn, lets loose the lower instincts. You can see it happening in the social life of Eastern Europe, where, through Leninism and Trotskyism, an attempt was made to establish the rule of the phrase. This, of course, can never work creatively and in Soviet Russia, therefore, the worst instincts have risen from the lower regions. For the same reason, instincts have risen up and come to the fore in our own younger generation. Such instincts are not even unhealthy in every respect, but they show that the older generation has been unable to endow language with the necessary soul qualities. Basically, the problems presented by our young are consequences of problems within the adult world; at least when regarded in a certain light,[4] they are parents' problems.

When meeting the young, we create all too easily an impression of being frightfully clever, making them feel frightfully stupid, whereas those who are able to learn from children are mostly the wisest people. If one does not approach the young with empty phrases, one meets them in a totally different way. The relationship between the younger generation and the adult world reflects our not having given it sufficient warmth of soul. This has contributed to their present character. That we must not blame everything that has gone wrong entirely on the younger generation becomes clearly evident, dear friends, by their response to what is being done for our young people in the Waldorf school, even during the short time of its existence.

And what was the result, or rather what was the cause, of our having lost the spirit in our spoken words? Today, you will find that what you read in innumerable articles and books basically consists of words spilling more or less automatically from the human soul. If one is open-minded and conversant with the current situation, one often needs to read no more than the first few lines or pages of an article or book in order to know what the author is thinking about the various points in question. The rest follows almost automatically out of the words themselves.

---

4. See CW 36 in the Collected Works of Rudolf Steiner, essays from 1923-1925.

Once the spirit has gone out of life, the result is an empty phrase-bound, cliché-ridden language, and this is what so often happens in today's cultural life. When people speak about cultural or spiritual matters or when they wish to participate in the cultural spiritual sphere of life, it is often no longer the living spirit that speaks through their being. It is clichés that dominate their language. This is true not only of how individuals express themselves. We find it above all in our "glorious" state education. Only think for a moment of how little of real substance is to be found in one or another political party that offers the most persuasive slogans or "party-phrases." People become intoxicated by these clichés. Slogans might to some degree satisfy the intellect, but party phrases will not grasp real life. And so it must be said that what we find when we reach the heights of agnosticism—which has already penetrated deeply into our society—is richly saturated with empty phrases. Living so closely with such clichés, we no longer feel a need for what is truly living in language. Words no longer rise from profound enough depths of the human soul. Change will occur only if we permeate ourselves with the spirit once more.

Two weeks ago, I wrote an article for *The Goetheanum* under the heading, "Spiritual Life Is Buried Alive." In it, I drew attention to the sublime quality of the writing that can still be found among authors who wrote around the middle of the nineteenth century. Only very few people are aware of this. I showed several people some of these books that looked as if they had been read almost continually for about a decade, after which they seemed to have been consigned to dust. Full of surprise, they asked me, "Where did you find those books?" I explained that I am in the habit, now and then, of poring over old books in second-hand bookshops. In those bookshops, I consult the appropriate catalogs and ask for certain chosen books to be delivered to wherever I am staying. In that way I manage to find totally forgotten books of all kinds, books that will never be reprinted but that give clear evidence of how the spirit has been "buried alive" in our times, at least to a certain extent.

As you have seen already, Waldorf education is primarily a question of finding the right teachers. I must confess that whenever I come to Stuttgart to visit and assist in the guidance of the Waldorf school—which unfortunately happens only seldom—I ask the same question in each class, naturally within the appropriate context and avoiding any possible tedium, "Children, do you love your teachers?" You should hear and witness the enthusiasm with which they call out in chorus, "Yes!" This call to the teachers to engender love within their pupils is all part of the question of how the older generation should relate to the young. In this context, it seems appropriate to mention that we decided from the beginning to open a complete primary school, comprising all eight classes in order to cover the entire age range of an elementary school.[5] And sometimes, when entering the school building, one could feel quite alarmed at the apparent lack of discipline, especially during break times. Those who jump to judgment too quickly said, "You see what a free Waldorf school is like! The pupils lose all sense of discipline." What they did not realize was that the pupils who had come to us from other schools had been brought up under so-called "iron discipline." Actually, they have already calmed down considerably but, when they first arrived under the influence of their previous "iron discipline," they were real scamps. The only ones who were moderately well-behaved were the first graders who had come directly from their parental homes—and even then, this was not always the case. Nevertheless, whenever I visit the Waldorf school, I notice a distinct improvement in discipline. And now, after a little more than two years of exist-

5. Six to fourteen.

ence, one can see a great change. Our pupils certainly won't turn into "apple-polishers" but they know that, if something goes wrong, they can always approach their teachers and trust them to enter into the matter sympathetically. This makes the pupils ready to confide. They may be noisy and full of boisterous energy—they certainly are not inhibited—but they are changing, and what can be expected in matters of discipline is gradually evolving. What I called in my lecture a natural sense of authority is also steadily growing.

For example, it is truly reassuring to hear the following report. A pupil entered the Waldorf school. He was already fourteen years old and was therefore placed into our top class. When he arrived, he was a thoroughly discontented boy who had lost all faith in his previous school. Obviously, a new school cannot offer a panacea to such a boy in the first few days. The Waldorf school must be viewed as a whole — if you were to cut a small piece from a painting, you could hardly give a sound judgment on the whole painting. There are people, for instance, who believe that they know all about the Waldorf school after having visited it for only one or two days. This is nonsense. One cannot become fully acquainted with the methods of anthroposophy merely by sampling a few of them. One must experience the spirit pervading the whole work. And so it was for the disgruntled boy who entered our school so late in the day. Naturally, what he encountered there during the first few days could hardly give him the inner peace and satisfaction for which he was hoping. After some time, however, he approached his history teacher, who had made a deep impression on him. The boy wanted to speak with this teacher, to whom he felt he could open his heart and tell of his troubles. This conversation brought about a complete change in the boy. Such a thing is only possible through the inner sense of authority of which I have spoken. These things become clear when this matter-of-fact authority has arisen by virtue of the quality of the teachers and their teaching. I don't think that I am being premature in saying that the young people who are now passing through the Waldorf school are hardly likely to exhibit the spirit of non-cooperation with the older generation of which the previous speaker spoke. It is really up to the teachers to play their parts in directing the negative aspects of the "storm and stress" fermenting in our youth into the right channels.

In the Waldorf school, we hold regular teacher meetings that differ substantially from those in other schools. During those meetings, each child is considered in turn and is discussed from a psychological point of view. All of us have learned a very great deal during these two years of practicing Waldorf pedagogy. This way of educating the young has truly grown into one organic whole.

We would not have been able to found our Waldorf school if we had not been prepared to make certain compromises. Right at the beginning, I drafted a memorandum that was sent to the education authorities. In it, we pledged to bring our pupils in their ninth year up to the generally accepted standards of learning, thus enabling them to enter another school if they so desired. The same generally accepted levels of achievement were to be reached in their twelfth and again in their fourteenth year. But, regarding our methods of teaching, we requested full freedom for the intervening years. This does constitute a compromise, but one must work within the given situation. It gave us the possibility of putting into practice what we considered to be essential for a healthy and right way of teaching. As an example, consider the case of school reports. From my childhood reports I recall certain phrases, such as "almost praiseworthy," "hardly satisfactory" and so on. But I never succeeded in discovering the wisdom behind my teachers' distinction of a "hardly satisfactory" from an "almost satisfactory" mark. You must bear with me, but this is exactly how it was. In the Waldorf school, instead of such stereotyped phrases or numerical marks, we write reports in which teachers express in their own style how each pupil has fared during the year. Our reports do not contain abstract remarks that must seem like mere empty phrases to the child. For, if something makes no sense, it is a mere phrase. As each child gradually grows up into life, the teachers write in their school reports what each pupil needs to know about him- or herself. Each report thus contains its own individual message, representing a kind of biography of the pupil's life at school during the previous school year. Furthermore, we end our reports with a little verse, specially composed for each child, epitomizing the year's progress. Naturally, writing this kind of report demands a great deal of time. But the child receives a kind of mirror of itself. So far, I have not come across a single student who did not show genuine interest in his or her report, even if it contained some real home truths. Especially the aptly chosen verse at the end is something that can become of real educational value to the child. One must make use of all means possible to call forth in the children the feeling that their guides and educators have taken the task of writing these reports very seriously, and that they have done so not in a one-sided manner, but from a direct and genuine interest in their charges. A great deal depends on our freeing ourselves from the cliché-ridden cultivation of the phrase so characteristic of our times, and on our showing the right kind of understanding for the younger generation. I am well aware that this is also connected with psychological predispositions of a more national character, and to gain mastery over these is an even more difficult task.

It might surprise you to hear that in none of the various anthroposophical conferences that we have held during the past few months was there any lack of younger members. They were always there and I never minced my words when speaking to them. But they soon realized that I was not addressing them with clichés or empty phrases. Even if they heard something very different from what they had expected, they could feel that what I said came straight from the heart, as all words of real value do. During our last conference in Stuttgart in particular, a number of young persons representing the youth movement were again present and, after a conversation with them lasting some one-and-a-half or two hours, it was unanimously decided to actually found an anthroposophical youth group, and this despite the fact that young people do not usually value anything even vaguely connected with authority, for they believe that everything has to grow from within, out of themselves, a principle that they were certainly not prepared to abandon.

What really matters is how the adults meet the young, how they approach them. From experience — many times confirmed — I can only point out that this whole question of the younger generation is often a question of the older generation. As such, it can perhaps be best answered by looking a little less at the younger generation and looking a little more deeply into ourselves.

*A Person From The Audience:* Perhaps, at this point, a member of the younger generation might be allowed to speak up. Please forgive my speaking plainly, but the truth is that we younger people have lost all respect for authority, for older people. Why? because our parents, too, have lost it. When talking to them or to other adults, we find that all that they can do is to criticize all kinds of unimportant, niggling things in others — thus showing their own generation in a bad light. We young people sometimes feel that those who are trying to educate us have become walking compromises, incapable of making up their minds on which side they stand, unable to state from the fullness of their hearts what their opinions are, unable to stand up for what they believe in. And we all the time have the feeling that our parents and educators do not in fact want to learn what we young are really like. Instead, they keep criticizing and condemning us. I need only to think of how we in our youth circle work together and what kind of things we study. For instance, we have read and discussed together Blüchner and Morgenstern. Just imagine those two polar opposites! This sort of thing happens with us all the time. Events in the world buffet us and nowhere can we find a center to give us a firm grasp. Nowhere can we find a really living person who can stand above it all with a comprehensive viewpoint—not even a person who can do so conceptually. How is it possible to teach unless behind everything that is taught there is a real living human being, whom one can feel coming through his or her teaching?... If that were to happen, it would rouse our enthusiasm. But, as long as our teachers do not approach us as human beings, as long as they are afraid even, sometimes, to laugh at themselves, we simply cannot feel the necessary confidence in them. I can say with complete conviction that we young people are really seeking adults to whom we can look up as authorities. We are looking for a center, for a firm grip with which we can pull ourselves up and that would enable us to grow into the kind of life that has an inner reality. That is why we throw ourselves into everything new that appears on the horizon: we always hope to discover something that could have a real meaning for us. But whenever this happens, we find nothing but a confusion of opinions and attitudes. We find judgments that are not real judgments at all, but are at best only criticisms.

If I may say something to the first speaker, who asked for a book to explain why young people behave as they do, I say: Don't read a book. To find an answer, read us young people! If you want to talk to the younger generation, you must approach them as living human beings. You must be ready to open yourself to them. Young people will then do the same and young and old will become clear about what each is looking for.

*Questioner:* As a teacher, I would like to ask Dr. Steiner whether he himself does not believe what the first speaker in today's discussion brought up; namely, that a quite new mood and spirit are stirring among young people today. This might perhaps be more evident in the larger cities, where even teachers with a deeply human attitude are no longer able to cope with difficulties as they were able to some fifty years ago. The source of the problem has been rightly sought in the older generation. Nevertheless, it cannot be denied that today's youth, under the influence of social-democratic ideas, is pervaded by skepticism to the extent that a teacher of Dr. Steiner's persuasion might not be able to imagine the kind of insolence and arrogance with which we have to put up. Socialistic contradictions are rife among the young, creating a false urge for independence in them that makes the teachers' tasks far more difficult than they were some time ago. Indeed, our job is now often almost impossible. What Dr. Steiner said gave the impression that the behavior of our youth merely reflects the shortcomings of their teachers. Certainly, teachers must take their share of the blame, but is it all the teachers' fault? Are all teachers to blame? That is the question. Is it not the case that the few good teachers, who are not to blame, nevertheless bluntly state that a new and different kind of youth has appeared and that lack of faith and skepticism among them makes the teacher's task far more difficult?

*Rudolf Steiner:* Well, if you put the question in this way, it is impossible to move forward. Putting it thus will not produce anything fruitful. It is the wrong way to begin. To declare that young people have changed and that it might have been easier to deal with them fifty years ago is not the point at all; the crux of the matter is to find ways and means of coping with the problem. After all, the younger generation is there, growing up in our midst. Nor is it productive to speak of our youth as being led into skepticism by social-democratic prejudices. That is as futile as if one were to criticize something in nature because it was growing in an undesirable way—and that is what is happening with the young. They are growing up among us like products of nature. Rather than stating the fact that the young have changed, and that perhaps it was easier to deal with them fifty years ago, the only way forward is to find ways and means of enabling the older generation to cooperate with the young again. We shall find no answer if we merely point out that today's youth is different from what it was fifty years ago, as if this were something to be accepted more or less fatalistically. That kind of attitude will never lead us to find an answer to this problem. Of course, the young have changed! And, if we observe life, we can see that the change has its positive aspects, too—that we could speak of it as a change toward something greater. Let me remind you, for instance, of the generational conflicts that we find expressed in literature. You can read them or see them performed on the stage. You still sometimes come across performances of plays from the late 1880s when the relationship between the younger and older generation was vividly portrayed. You will see that what we are discussing is an age-old problem. It has been regarded for centuries as a kind of catastrophe. By comparison, what is happening today is mere child's play! But, as I said before, merely to state facts will not lead us further.

The question everywhere is how to regain the lost respect for authority in individual human beings that will enable you as teachers and educators to find the right relationship to the young. That it is generally correct to state that young people do not find the necessary conditions for such a respect and sense of authority in the older generation and that they find among its members an attitude of compromise is in itself, in my opinion, no evidence against what I have said. This striving for compromise can be found on a much wider scale even in world events, so that the question of how to regain respect for human authority and dignity could be extended to a world-wide level. I would like to add that—of course—I realize that there exist good and devoted teachers as described by the last speaker. But the pupils usually behave differently when taught by those good teachers. If one discriminates, one can observe that the young respond quite differently in their company.

We must not let ourselves be led into an attitude of complaining and doubting by judgments that are too strongly colored by our own hypotheses, but must be clear that ultimately the way in which the younger generation behaves is, in general, conditioned by the older generation. My observations were not meant to imply that teachers were to be held solely responsible for the faults of the young. At this point, I feel rather tempted to point to how lack of respect for authority is revealed in its worst light when we look at some of the events of recent history. Only remember certain moments during the last, catastrophic war. There was a need to replace older, leading personalities. What kind of person was chosen? In France, Clemenceau, in Germany, Hertling—all old men of the most ancient kind who carried a certain authority only because they had once been important personalities. But they were no longer the kind of person who could take his or her stance from a direct grasp of the then current situation. And what is happening now? Only recently the prime ministers of three leading countries found their positions seriously jeopardized. Yet all three are still in office, simply because no other candidate could be found who carried sufficient weight of authority! That was the only reason for their survival as prime ministers. And so we find that, in important world happenings, too, a general sense of authority has been undermined, even in leading figures. You can hardly blame the younger generation for that! But these symptoms have a shattering effect on the young who witness them.

We really have to tackle this whole question at a deeper level and, above all, in a more positive light. We must be clear that, instead of complaining about the ways in which the young confront their elders, we should be thinking of how we can improve our own attitude toward young. To continue telling them how wrong they are and that it is no longer possible to cooperate with them can never lead to progress. In order to work toward a more fruitful future, we must look for what the spiritual cultural sphere, and life in general, can offer to help us regain respect and trust in the older generation. Those who know the young know that they are only too happy when they can have faith in their elders again. This is really true. Their skepticism ceases as soon as they can find something of real value, something in which they can believe. Generally speaking, we cannot yet say that life is ruled by what is right. But, if we offer our youth something true, they will feel attracted to it. If we no longer believe this to be the case, if all that we do is moan and groan about youth's failings, then we shall achieve nothing at all.

# 3

# A Lecture to English Educators

LONDON — AUGUST 29, 1924

FIRST OF ALL I would like to express my heartfelt thanks to Mrs. Mackenzie for her kind words of greeting, and to all of you who have made the effort to meet again, at Professor Mackenzie's invitation, to discuss questions of education. In the short time available little can be said about the educational methods based on anthroposophy, for their essence is in an educational practice that does not have fixed programs, nor clearly defined general concepts to encompass it. The main intention of Waldorf education is that its teachers should be able to look deeply into the nature of the child from a true and genuine knowledge of the human being, and that in the individuality of each child who has come down into the earthly realm, they should be able to experience a wondrous enigma, which the educator and the world can never hope to understand completely.

The teacher's practical task is to discern ways to approach the mystery, the enigma, that divine guiding spirits present us with each child who joins our contemporary society. The teacher's task begins at the age when the child discards the baby teeth, around the seventh year, and extends until the eighteenth or nineteenth year when, as a young man or woman, the student either goes out into life or enters higher education.

A few years ago, due to the devastating war, many new ideals, and certainly many illusions as well, emerged in Germany. At that time, the industrialist Emil Molt saw an opportunity to do something important for the workers in his factory. He felt that, by opening a school for their children, he could to some extent help reconcile his workers with their destiny as factory workers, and above all do something about what was then the great social demand of the time—he wanted to begin a school for his employees' children, where the children, although laborers' children, would get the best possible education imaginable.

This should make it clear immediately that the education I am representing here was not hatched from some ideas or from any plan for reform; it was, instead, born as a direct answer to a practical life situation. Emil Molt simply declared, "My workers have a total of a hundred and fifty children, and these children must be educated in the best way possible." This could happen within the anthroposophical movement because, as strange as it may sound to you, anthroposophists are neither theorists nor visionary dreamers, but practical people who take the pragmatic side of life seriously; indeed, we like to believe that practical matters are nurtured especially within the anthroposophical movement. In other words, the idea regarding this education was the direct result of a practical need.

In Stuttgart, where all this happened, the necessary conditions for starting such a school were soon created. At that time, a democratic legislation of schools did not yet exist; that came into force only with the subsequent democratically constituted assembly. We came just in time to begin the school before the emergence of a "free" school legislation,

which forced a general levelling of all schools in Germany—
paying lip service to freedom by enforcing fixed laws. So we
were only just in time to open such a school. I must quickly
add that the school authorities have always shown great
understanding and cooperation ever since the school was
founded. It was fortunately possible to begin "The Free
Waldorf School" in complete freedom. Its name arose because
of its association with the Waldorf-Astoria Factory.

I do not wish to imply in any way that state-trained
teachers are inferior, and certainly not that they are poor
teachers simply because they have passed a state exam!
Nevertheless, I was granted freedom in my choice of teachers,
regardless of whether they were state trained or not. It was left
to my discretion whether my candidates would make good
and efficient teachers, and it happens that most of the
teachers at the Waldorf school, based on the educational
principles I wish to speak about, are in fact not state trained.

However, the situation did not remain as it was then. The
school was begun with a hundred and fifty students. In no
time at all, anthroposophists living in Stuttgart also wanted to
send their children to this school because the education it
offered was supposed to be very good. Since then (only a few
years ago) the school has grown to more than eight hundred
children. Several grades, like our fifth and sixth grades, have
three parallel classes.

A further step, perhaps not quite as practical (I don't want
to judge this) was that Emil Molt, after deciding to open the
school, asked me to provide the school with spiritual guidance
and methods. It was only possible to give this guidance based
on the spiritual research and knowledge of the human being
that I represent. Our fundamental goal is to know the
complete human being as a being of body, soul, and spirit, as
a person grows from childhood, and to be able to read in the
soul of the child what needs to be done each week, month,

and year. Consequently, one could say our education is a teaching based entirely on knowledge of the child, and this knowledge guides us in finding the appropriate methods and principles.

I can give only general and sketchy outlines here of what is meant by knowledge of the human being. There is much talk nowadays about physical education, about the importance of not sacrificing physical education to the education of the child's mind and soul. However, to separate the physical aspect from that of the soul and spirit is in itself a great illusion, because in a young child, spirit, soul, and body form a unity. It is impossible to separate one realm from the other in early childhood.

To give an example, let us imagine a child at school; a child becomes more and more pale. The paling of the child is a physical symptom that the teacher should notice. If an adult becomes increasingly pale, one seeks the advice of a doctor, who will think of an appropriate therapy according to an understanding of the case. Teachers of an abnormally pale child must ask themselves whether this child was already that pale when entering the class, or if the child's complexion changed afterward. Lo and behold, they may realize that they themselves were the cause of the child's pallor, because of excessive demands on the child's memory forces. Consequently they will realize that they must reduce the pressure in this respect. Here is a case where physical symptoms reveal problems in the sphere of the soul. The child becomes pale because the memory has been overtaxed.

Then again, teachers may be faced with a different type of child; this time the child does not turn pale; on the contrary, the complexion becomes increasingly ruddy. This child appears to lack good will, gets restless, and turns into what is usually called a "hyperactive" child. The child lacks discipline, jumps up and down and cannot sit still for a moment, constantly wanting to run in and out. It is now up to the teacher to find the cause of these changes, and, lo and behold, it may be found (not always, because individual cases vary greatly and have to be diagnosed individually) that the child had been given too little to remember. This can easily happen because the appropriate amount of material to be remembered varies greatly from child to child.

As it happens, government inspectors visit our school. The authorities make sure that they know what is happening in our school! At the time when socialism was flourishing, one local director of education came to inspect the school, and I took him around to the various classes for three days. I pointed out that our physical education was intended to develop the students' spiritual capacities, and that we educate their mental-spiritual capacities in such a way that their physical bodies benefit, because the two form a unity. Thereupon the inspector exclaimed, "But in this case your teachers would have to know medicine as well, and that is not possible!" To which I answered, "I do not think so, but if it were indeed necessary, it would have to be done, because a teacher's training must ensure that the teacher is capable of thorough insight into the physical and spiritual background of the growing child."

Furthermore, if one has a child of the type just described, a child who becomes increasingly restless and who does not become pale but, on the contrary, becomes flushed, one can think of all kinds of things to do. However, to help such a child, one has to make sure of the right treatment. And the right treatment may be very difficult to find, for insight into human nature must not limit its considerations to a certain period of time, such as from age seven to age fourteen, which is the time when the class teacher is with the children. One must realize that much of what happens during these seven years has consequences that manifest only much later. One might choose the comfortable ways of experimental psychology, which only considers the child's present state of development to decide what to do, but if one endeavors to survey the child's whole life from birth to death, one knows: When I give the child too little content to remember, I induce a tendency toward serious illness, which may not appear before the forty-fifth year; I may cause a layer of fat to form above the heart. One has to know what form of illness may be induced eventually through the education of the child's soul and spirit. Knowledge of the human being is not confined to an experiment with a student in the present condition, but includes knowledge of the whole human being—body, soul, and spirit—as well as a knowledge of what happens during various ages and stages of life.

When these matters become the basis for teaching, one will also find them relevant in the moral sphere. You may agree with me when I say that there are some people who, in ripe old age, give off an atmosphere of blessing to those in their company. They needn't say much, but nevertheless radiate beneficial influence to others merely by the expression in their eyes, their mere presence, arm gestures— saying little perhaps, but speaking with a certain intonation and emphasis, or a characteristic tempo. They can permeate whatever they say or do with love, and this is what creates the effect of blessing on those around them. What kind of people are they?

In order to explain this phenomenon with real insight into human life, one must look back to their childhood. One then finds that such people learned, in their childhood, to revere and pray to the spiritual world in the right way, for no one has the gift of blessing in old age who has not learned to fold his or her hands in prayer between the ages of seven and fourteen. This folding of the hands in prayer during the age of primary education enters deeply into the inner organization of the human being and is transformed into the capacity for blessing in old age. This example shows how different life stages are interrelated and interwoven in human life. When educating children, one educates for all of life—that is, during a person's younger years one may cultivate possibilities for moral development in old age.

This education does not encroach on human freedom. Human freedom is attacked primarily when a certain inner resistance struggles against a free will impulse. What I have been talking about is connected with freeing a person from inner impediments and hindrances.

This should suffice as an introduction to tonight's theme. When one tries to achieve a more intimate knowledge of human nature, observing it not just externally but also with the inner gaze directed more toward the spiritual, one discovers that human beings pass through clearly defined life periods.

The first three periods of life are of particular importance and interest for education. The first one has a more homogeneous character and lasts from birth to age seven— that is, until the time of the change of teeth. The second period of life extends from the change of teeth to puberty, around age fourteen. The third begins at puberty and ends in the twenties. It is easy to notice external physical changes, but only a trained capacity for observation will reveal the more hidden aspects of these different life periods.

Such observation shows that during the first seven years, roughly from birth to the change of teeth, the child's spirit, soul, and body are completely merged into a unity. Observe a child entering into this world, with open features still undifferentiated, movements uncoordinated, and without the ability to show even the most primitive human expressions, such as laughing or weeping. (A baby can cry, of course, but this crying is not really weeping; it does not spring from emotions of the soul because the soul realm has not yet developed independently.) All of this makes the child into a unique being, and indeed, the greatest wonder of the world. We observe a baby weekly and monthly; from an undefined physiognomy, something gradually evolves in the physical configuration of the little body, as if coming from a center. Soul qualities begin to animate not only the child's looks, but also the hand and arm movements. And it is a wonderful moment when, after moving about on hands and knees, the child for the first time assumes the vertical posture. To anyone who can observe this moment, it appears as a most wonderful phenomenon.

When we perceive all this with spiritual awareness, which can be done, it shows us the following: There, in this unskillful little body, spirit is living, spirit that cannot yet control limb movements. This is still done very clumsily, but it is the same human spirit that, later on, may develop into a genius. It is there, hidden in the movements of arms and legs, in questing facial expression, and in the searching sense of taste.

Then we find that, from birth until the second dentition, the young child is almost entirely one sense organ. What is the nature of a sense organ? It surrenders fully to the world. Consider the eye. The entire visible world is mirrored in the eye and is contained in it. The eye is totally surrendered to the world. Likewise the child, though in a different way, is surrendered fully to the environment. We adults may taste sweet, bitter, or acid tastes on the tongue and with the palate, but the tastes do not penetrate our entire organism. Although we are not usually aware of it, it is nevertheless true to say that when the baby drinks milk the taste of the milk is allowed to permeate the entire organism. The baby lives completely like an eye, like one large sense organ. The differentiation between outer and inner senses occurs only later. And the characteristic feature is that, when a child perceives something, it is done in a state of dreamy consciousness.

If, for example, a very choleric father, a man who in behaviors, gestures, and attitudes is always ready to lose his temper, and displays the typical symptoms of his temperament around a child, then the child, in a dreaming consciousness, perceives not only the outer symptoms, but also the father's violent temperament. The child does not recognize temperamental outbursts as such, but perceives the underlying disposition, and this perception directly affects the finest vascular vessels right into the blood circulation and respiration. The young child's physical and bodily existence is thus affected immediately by the spiritual impressions received. We may admonish a child, we may say all kinds of things, but until the seventh year this is all meaningless to the child. The only thing that matters is how we ourselves act and behave in its presence. Until the change of teeth, a child is entirely an imitating being, and upbringing and education can be effected only by setting the proper example to be imitated. This is the case for moral matters as well.

In such matters one can have some rather strange experiences. One day a father of a young child came to me in a state of great agitation because (so he told me) his son, who had always been such a good boy, had stolen! The father was very confused, because he was afraid this was a sign that his son would develop into a morally delinquent person. I said to him, "Let's examine first whether your son has really stolen. What has he actually done?" "He has taken money out of the cupboard from which his mother takes money to pay household expenses. With this money he bought sweets, which he gave to other children." I could reassure the father that his boy had not stolen at all, that the child had merely imitated what he had seen his mother do several times every day. Instinctively he had imitated his mother, taking money out of the cupboard, because Mother had been doing it.

Whether in kindergarten or at home, we educate the child only when we base all education and child rearing on the principle of imitation, which works until the second dentition. Speaking, too, is learned purely by imitation. Up to the change of teeth, a child learns everything through imitation. The only principle necessary at this stage is that human behavior should be worthy of imitation. This includes also thinking, because in their own way, children perceive whether our thoughts are moral or not. People do not usually believe in these imponderables, but they are present nevertheless. While around young children, we should not allow ourselves even a single thought that is unworthy of being absorbed by the child.

These things are all connected directly with the child as an imitator until the change of teeth. Until then all possibility of teaching and bringing up a child depends on recognizing this principle of imitation. There is no need to consider whether we should introduce one or another Froebel kindergarten method, because everything that has been contrived in this field belongs to the age of materialism. Even when we work with children according to the Froebel system, it is not the actual content of the work that influences them, but how we do it. Whatever we ask children to do without doing it first ourselves in front of them is merely extra weight that we impose on them.

The situation changes when the child's change of teeth begins. During this stage the primary principle of early education is the teacher's natural authority. Acceptance of authority is spontaneous on the child's part, and it is not necessary to enforce it in any way. During the first seven years of life a child will copy what we do. During the second seven years, from the change of teeth until puberty, a child is guided and oriented by what those in authority bring through their own conduct and through their words. This relationship has nothing to do with the role of freedom in human life in a social and individual sense, but it has everything to do with the nature of the child between the second dentition and puberty. At this point it is simply part of a child's nature to want to look up with natural respect to the authority of a revered teacher who represents all that is right and good. Between the seventh and fourteenth years, a child still cannot judge objectively whether something is true, good, or beautiful; therefore only through the guidance of a naturally respected authority can the students find their bearings in life. Advocating the elimination of a child's faith in the teacher's authority at this particular age would actually eliminate any real and true education.

Why does a child of this age believe something is true? Because the authority of the teacher and educator says so. The teacher is the source of truth. Why does something appeal to a child of this age as beautiful? Because the teacher reveals it as such. This also applies to goodness. At this age children have to gain abstract judgment of truth, goodness, and beauty by experiencing concretely the judgments of those in authority. Everything depends on whether the adult in charge exerts a self-evident authority on the child between seven and fourteen; for now the child is no longer a sense organ but has developed a soul that needs nourishment in the form of images or thoughts. We now have to introduce all teaching subjects imaginatively, pictorially—that is, artistically. To do so, teachers need the gift of bringing everything to children at this age in the form of living pictures.

But what does the sign we write on the paper have to do with this sound? The child has no inner relationship to what has now become modern abstract writing. If we return to earlier civilizations, we find that writing was different then. In the ancient days, people painted what they wished to express. Look at Egyptian hieroglyphics—they have a direct relationship to the human soul. When introducing writing to the child, we must return to expressing what we wish to communicate in the form of pictures. This is possible, however, only when we do not begin by introducing the alphabet directly, nor reading as a subject, but when we start with painting. As teachers, we ourselves must be able to live in a world of imagery. For example, let's imagine that we have to teach a young child to read. Consider what this implies—the child is expected to decipher signs written or printed on paper. In this form they are completely alien to the child. Sounds, speech, and vowels that carry a person's feelings and are inwardly experienced, are not alien to the child. A child knows the sense of wonder felt at seeing the sun rise. "Ah" (*A*) is the sound of wonder. The sound is there, but what does the sign that we write on paper have to do with it? The child knows the feeling of apprehension of something uncanny: "Oo" (*U*).

Consequently, when young students enter our school, we introduce them first to the world of flowing colors with watercolor painting. Naturally, this can cause a certain amount of chaos and disorder in the classroom, but the teacher copes with that. The children learn how to work with paints, and through the use of color the teacher can guide them toward definite forms. With the necessary skill, the teacher can allow the shapes of the letters to evolve from such painted forms. In this way, the children gain a direct relationship to the various shapes of the letters. It is possible to develop the written vowels *A* or *U* so that first one paints the mood of wonder (or of fright), finally allowing the picture to assume the form of the appropriate letters.

All teaching must have an artistic quality based on the pictorial element. The first step is to involve the whole being of the child in the effort of painting, which is subsequently transformed into writing. Only later do we develop the faculty of reading, which is linked to the head system—that is, to only one part of the human being. Reading comes after writing. First a form of drawing with paint (leading the child from color experience to form), out of which writing is evolved. Only then do we introduce reading.

The point is that, from the nature of the child, the teacher should learn how to proceed. This is the right way of finding the appropriate method, based on one's observation and knowledge of the child. Our Waldorf school has to do with method, not theory. It always endeavors to solve the wonderful riddle, the riddle of the growing child, and to introduce to the child what the child's own nature is bringing to the surface. In using this method, one finds that between the second dentition and puberty one has to approach all teaching pictorially and imaginatively, and this is certainly possible.

Yet, in order to carry the necessary authority, one has to have the right attitude toward what one's pictures really represent. For example, it is possible to speak to one's students even at a relatively early age about the immortality of the human soul. (In giving this example, I am not trying to solve a philosophical problem, but speak only from the perspective of practical pedagogy.) One could say to a child, "Look at the cocoon and its shape." One should show it to a child if possible. "You see, the cocoon opens and a butterfly flies out! This is how it is when a human being dies. The human body is like the cocoon of a butterfly. The soul flies out of the body, even though we cannot see it. When someone dies, just as the butterfly flies out of the cocoon, so the soul flies out of the body into the spiritual world."

Now, there are two possible ways that a teacher can introduce this simile. In one instance, the teacher may feel very superior to the "ignorant" student, considering oneself clever and the child ignorant. But this attitude does not accomplish much. If, in creating a picture for the child, one thinks that one is doing so only to help the child understand the abstract concept of immortality, such a picture will not convey much, because imponderables play a role. Indeed, the child will gain nothing unless the teacher is convinced of the truth of this picture, feeling that one is involved with something sacred. Those who can look into the spiritual world believe in the truth of this picture, because they know that, with the emerging butterfly, divine-spiritual powers have pictured in the world the immortality of the human soul. Such people know this image to be true and not a teacher's concoction for the benefit of "ignorant" students. If teachers feel united with this picture, believing what they have put into it and thus identifying themselves with it, they will be real and natural authorities for their students. Then the child is ready to accept much, although it will appear fruitful only later in life.

It has become popular to present everything in simple and graphic form so that "even children can understand it." This results in appalling trivialities. One thing, however, is not considered. Let's assume that, when the teacher stands before the child as the representative and source of truth, beauty, and goodness, a child of seven accepts something on the teacher's authority, knowing that the teacher believes in it. The child cannot yet understand the point in question because the necessary life experience has not occurred. Much later—say, at the age of thirty five—life may bring something like an "echo," and suddenly the former student realizes that long ago the teacher spoke about the same thing, which only now, after having gained a great deal more life experience, can be understood fully.

In this way a bridge is made between the person who was eight or nine years old, and the person who is now thirty-five years old, and this has a tremendously revitalizing effect on such a person, granting a fresh increase of life forces. This fact is well-known to anyone with a deep knowledge of the human being, and education must be built on such knowledge.

Through using our educational principles in the Waldorf school in this and similar ways, we endeavor to attune our education of body, soul, and spirit to the innermost core of the child's being. For example, there might be a phlegmatic child in a class. We pay great attention to the children's temperaments, and we even arrange the seating order in the classrooms according to temperaments. Consequently we put the phlegmatic children into one group. This is not only convenient for the teachers, because they are always aware of where their young phlegmatics are sitting, but it also has a beneficial effect on the children themselves, in that the phlegmatics who sit together bore each other to death with their indifference. By overcoming some of their temperament, they become a little more balanced.

As for the cholerics who constantly push and punch each other when sitting together, they learn in a wonderfully corrective way how to curb their temperament, at least to some extent! And so it goes. If teachers know how to deal with the various temperaments by assuming, let us say, a thoroughly phlegmatic attitude themselves when dealing with phlegmatic children, they cause in these little phlegmatics a real inner disgust with their own temperament.

Such things must become a part of our teaching, in order to turn it into a really artistic task. It is especially important for students at this age. Teachers may have a melancholic child in their class. If they can look into the spiritual background, in an anthroposophical sense, they may want to find and think through some measure for the benefit of such a child. The education we speak of begins with the knowledge that spirit exists in everything of a physical-bodily nature. One cannot see through matter, but one can learn to know it by seeing its spiritual counterpart, thereby discovering the nature of matter. Materialism suffers from ignorance of what matter really is, because it does not see the spirit in matter.

To return to our little melancholic, such a student can cause us serious concern. The teacher might feel prompted to come up with very ingenious ideas to help the child overcome a particularly melancholic temperament. This, however, can often prove fruitless. Although such a situation may have been observed very correctly, the measures taken may not lead to the desired effect. If, on the other hand, teachers realize that a deterioration of the liver function is at the root of this melancholic nature, if they suspect that there is something wrong with the child's liver, they will know the course of action necessary. They must contact the child's parents and find out as much as possible about the child's eating habits. In this way they may discover that the little melancholic needs to eat more sugar. The teachers try to win the parents' cooperation, because they know from spiritual science that the beginnings of a degeneration in the liver function connected with melancholia can be overcome by an increased sugar intake. If they succeed in gaining the parents' help, they will have taken the right step from an educational perspective. It would be necessary to know, through spiritual insight, that an increase of sugar consumption can heal or balance a pathological liver condition.

One must be able to perceive and know the growing child and even the individual organs. This is fundamental in our education. We do not insist on particular external circumstances for our schooling. Whether forest or heath, town or country, our opinion is that one can succeed in a fruitful education within any existing social conditions, as long as one really understands the human being deeply, and if, above all, one knows how the child develops.

These are only a few criteria that I may speak of today, which characterize the nature of Waldorf education and the methods used for its implementation, all of which are based on a spiritual-scientific foundation.

If one can approach the child's being in this way, the necessary strength is found to help children develop both physically and morally, so that fundamental moral forces manifest also. Barbaric forms of punishment are unnecessary, because the teacher's natural authority will ensure the proper inner connection between teacher and child. Wonderful things can happen in our Waldorf school to demonstrate this. For example, the following incident occurred a little while ago: Among our teachers there was one who imported all kinds of customary disciplinary measures from conventional school life into the Waldorf school. When a few children were naughty, he thought he would have to keep them in after school. He told them that they would have to stay behind as punishment and do some extra work in arithmetic. Spontaneously, the whole class pleaded to be allowed to stay behind and do arithmetic as well, because, as they called out, "Arithmetic is such fun!" What better things could they do than additional work in arithmetic? "We too want to be kept in," they declared. Well, here you have an example of what can happen in the Waldorf school where teachers have implanted in their students the right attitude toward work. The teacher of course had to learn his own lesson: One must never use something that should be considered a reward as a punishment. This example is one of many that could be mentioned. It shows how one can create a real art of education based on knowledge of the human being.

I am extremely thankful to Mrs. Mackenzie for giving me the opportunity of at least outlining just some of the fundamentals of education based upon anthroposophical spiritual science. Our teaching is based on definite methods, and not on vague ideals born of mere fantasy. These methods answer the needs and demands of human nature and are the primary justification for our education. We do not believe in creating ideas of what ideal human beings should be so that they fit into preconceived plans. Our goal is to be able to observe children realistically, to hear the message sent to us through the children from the divine-spiritual worlds. We wish to feel the children's inner affirmation of our picture of the human being. God, speaking through the child, says: "This is how I wish to become."

We try to fulfil this call for the child through our educational methods in the best way possible. Through our art of education, we try to supply a positive answer to this call.

# Further Reading

Most of the following books, as well as many others on education and child development, are available through SteinerBooks, 610 Main Street, Great Barrington, MA 01230. Request our free SteinerBooks Education Catalog, or visit our website www.steinerbooks.org.

## Rudolf Steiner: Lectures and Writings on Education

*Balance in Teaching,* Anthroposophic Press, 2007.

*The Child's Changing Consciousness As the Basis of Pedagogical Practice,* Anthroposophic Press, 1996.

*Discussions with Teachers,* includes the "Curriculum Lectures," Anthroposophic Press, 1997.

*Education and Modern Spiritual Life,* Garber Publications, 1989.

*Education as a Force for Social Change,* previously *Education as a Social Problem,* Anthroposophic Press, 1997.

*Education for Adolescents,* previously *The Supplementary Course— Upper School and Waldorf Education for Adolescence,* Anthroposophic Press, 1996.

*Education for Special Needs: The Curative Education Course,* Rudolf Steiner Press, 1999.

*The Education of the Child and Early Lectures on Education,* Anthroposophic Press, 1996.

*The Essentials of Education,* Anthroposophic Press, 1997.

*Faculty Meetings with Rudolf Steiner,* 2 volumes, Anthroposophic Press, 1998.

*The Foundations of Human Experience,* previously *Study of Man,* Anthroposophic Press, 1996.

*The Genius of Language,* Anthroposophic Press, 1995.

*Human Values in Education,* Anthroposophic Press, 2005.

*The Kingdom of Childhood,* Anthroposophic Press, 1995.

*The Light Course—First Course in Natural Science: Light, Color, Sound, Mass, Electricity, Magnetism,* Anthroposophic Press, 2001.

*A Modern Art of Education*, Anthroposophic Press, 2003.

*Observations on Adolescence: The Third Phase of Human Development,* The Association of Waldorf Schools of North America, 2001.

*Practical Advice to Teachers,* Anthroposophic Press, 2000.

*"The Relation of the Diverse Branches of Natural Science to Astronomy"* (also known as *"The Astronomy Course"*) (available in typescript only).

*The Renewal of Education,* Anthroposophic Press, 2001.

*The Roots of Education,* Anthroposophic Press, 1997.

*Rudolf Steiner in the Waldorf School: Lectures and Conversations,* Anthroposophic Press, 1996.

*Soul Economy: Body Soul, and Spirit in Waldorf Education,* Anthroposophic Press, 2003.

*The Spirit of the Waldorf School,* Anthroposophic Press, 1995.

*The Spiritual Ground of Education,* Anthroposophic Press, 2003.

*Waldorf Education and Anthroposophy 1,* Anthroposophic Press, 1995.

*Waldorf Education and Anthroposophy 2*, Anthroposophic Press, 1996.

*The Warmth Course*, Mercury Press, 1988.

## Rudolf Steiner: Other Writings and Lectures

*Agriculture: Spiritual Foundations for the Renewal of Agriculture,* Bio-Dynamic Farming and Gardening Association, 1993.

*Anthroposophical Leading Thoughts: Anthroposophy as a Path of Knowledge and The Michael Mystery,* Rudolf Steiner Press, 1985.

*Anthroposophy (A Fragment),* Anthroposophic Press, 1996.

*Anthroposophy in Everyday Life,* Anthroposophic Press, 1995.

*Autobiography: Chapter in the Course of My Life,* SteinerBooks, 2006.

*The Boundaries of Natural Science,* Anthroposophic Press, 1983.

*The Calendar of the Soul,* Ruth & Hans Pusch, trans., Anthroposophic Press, 1988.

*Christianity as Mystical Fact,* SteinerBooks, 2006.

*Colour,* Rudolf Steiner Press, 1992.

*Curative Eurythmy,* Rudolf Steiner Press, 1983.

*Egyptian Myths and Mysteries,* Anthroposophic Press, 1997.

*Extending Practical Medicine,* coauthor with Dr. Ita Wegman, previously published as *Fundamentals of Therapy,* Rudolf Steiner Press, 1996.

*Eurythmy as Visible Music,* Rudolf Steiner Press, n.d.

*Eurythmy as Visible Speech,* Rudolf Steiner Press, 1984.

*The Foundation Stone / The Life, Nature, and Cultivation of Anthroposophy,* Rudolf Steiner Press, 1996.

*Founding A Science of the Spirit,* Rudolf Steiner Press, 1986.

*The Fruits of Anthroposophy,* Rudolf Steiner Press, 1986.

*How to Know Higher Worlds: A Modern Path of Initiation,* Christopher Bamford, trans., Anthroposophic Press, 1994.

*The Inner Nature of Music and the Experience of Tone,* Anthroposophic Press, 1983.

*An Introduction to Eurythmy,* Anthroposophic Press, 1984.

*Intuitive Thinking as a Spiritual Path: A Philosophy of Freedom,* Anthroposophic Press, 1995.

*An Outline of Esoteric Science,* Anthroposophic Press, 1997.

*A Psychology of Body, Soul and Spirit, Anthroposophic Press, 1998.*

*Prayers for Parents and Children,* Rudolf Steiner Press, 1995.

*Reincarnation and Karma: Two Fundamental Truths of Human Existence,* Anthroposophic Press, 1992.

*The Social Future,* Anthroposophic Press, 1972.

*Speech and Drama,* Anthroposophic Press, 1959.

*Start Now! Meditation Instruction, Meditations, Prayers, Verses for the Dead, Karma & Other Spiritual Practices,* SteinerBooks, 2003.

*The Spiritual Guidance of the Individual and Humanity,* Anthroposophic Press, 1992.

*Theosophy: An Introduction to the Spiritual Processes in Human Life and in the Cosmos,* Anthroposophic Press, 1994.

*Verses and Meditations,* Rudolf Steiner Press, 1993.

*What Is Anthroposophy?* Anthroposophic Press, 2003.

## Other Authors

Adams, George and Olive Whicher. *The Plant Between Sun and Earth,* Rudolf Steiner Press, 1980.

Aeppli, Willi. *The Developing Child: Sense and Nonsense in Education,* Anthroposophic Press, 2001.

Alcott, A. Bronson. *How Like An Angel Came I Down,* Lindisfarne Books, 1991.

Andersen, Henning. *Active Arithmetic! Movement and Mathematics Teaching in the Lower Grades of a Waldorf School,* The Association of Waldorf Schools of North America, 1995.

Anschutz, Marieka. *Children and Their Temperament,* Floris Books, 1995.

Auer, Arthur. *Learning about the World through Modeling: Sculptural Ideas for School and Home,* The Association of Waldorf Schools of North America, 2001.

Baldwin, Rahima. *You Are Your Child's First Teacher,* Celestial Arts, 1989.

Bamford, Christopher. *An Endless Trace: The Passionate Pursuit of Wisdom in the West,* Codhill Press, 2003.

Baravalle, Hermann von. *The Teaching of Arithmetic and the Waldorf School Plan,* Waldorf School Monographs, 1967.

—— *Introduction to Physics in the Waldorf Schools: The Balance Between Art and Science,* Waldorf School Monographs, 1967.

—— *Geometric Drawing and the Waldorf School Plan,* Waldorf School Monographs, 1969.

Barfield, Owen. *History in English Words,* Lindisfarne Books, 1967.

Barnes, Christy MacKaye, ed. *For the Love of Literature: A Celebration of Language and Imagination,* Anthroposophic Press, 1996.

Barnes, Henry. *A Life for the Spirit: Rudolf Steiner in the Crosscurrents of Our Time,* Anthroposophic Press, 1997.

Berger, Thomas & Petra. *Crafts through the Year,* Floris Books, 1999.

Bortoft, Henri. *The Wholeness of Nature: Goethe's Way toward a Science of Conscious Participation in Nature,* Lindisfarne Books, 1996.

Bott, Victor. *Spiritual Science and the Art of Healing,* Inner Traditions, 1984.

Burton, Michael Hedley. *In the Light of a Child,* Anthroposophic Press, 1989.

Capel, Evelyn Francis. *The Mystery of Growing Up,* Temple Lodge, 1990.

—— *Celebrating Festivals Around the World,* Temple Lodge, 1991.

Carey, Diana & Judy Large. *Festivals, Family and Food,* Hawthorn Press, 1982.

Childs, Gilbert. *Understand Your Temperament!* Rudolf Steiner Press, 1995.

—— *Rudolf Steiner: His Life and Work,* Anthroposophic Press, 1995.

—— *Steiner Education in Theory and Practice,* Floris Books, 1991.

Clark, F. and H. Kofsky and J. Lauruol. *To a Different Drumbeat: A Practical Guide for Parenting Children with Special Needs,* Hawthorn Press, 1981.

Clouder, Christopher & Martyn Rawson. *Waldorf Education: Rudolf Steiner's Ideas in Practice,* Floris Books, 2003.

Cooper, Stephanie, Christine Fynes-Clinton, Marye Rowling. *The Children's Year,* Hawthorn Press, 1986.

Coplen, Dotty Turner. *Parenting for a Healthy Future,* Hawthorn Press, 1995.

—— *Parenting a Path Through Childhood,* Floris Books, 1982.

Cook, Wendy. *Foodwise: Understanding What We Eat and How It Affects Us,* Rudolf Steiner Press, Clairview Books, 2003.

Davidson, Norman. *Sky Phenomena: A Guide to Naked Eye Observation of the Stars,* Lindisfarne Press, 1993.

Davy, Gudrun. *Lifeways,* Hawthorn Press, 1983.

De Haes Daniel Udo. *The Young Child: Creative Living with Two to Four-Year-Olds,* Floris Books, 1986.

Edelglas, Stephen and Georg Maier, Hans Gebert, and John Davy. *The Marriage of Sense and Thought: Imaginative Participation in Science,* Lindisfarne Press, 1997.

Edmonds, Francis. *Renewing Education,* Hawthorn Press, 1992.

Edwards, Lawrence. *The Vortex of Life: Nature's Patterns in Space and Time,* Floris Books, 1993.

Elium, Jeanne & Don. *Raising a Daughter: Parents and the Awakening of a Healthy Woman,* Celestial Arts, 1994.

—— *Raising a Son: Parents and the Making of a Healthy Man,* Celestial Arts, 1992.

—— *Raising a Family: Living on Planet Parenthood,* Celestial Arts, 1997.

Finser, Torin. *In Search of Ethical Leadership, If not now, when?* SteinerBooks, 2003.

—— *School Renewal: A Spiritual Journey for Change,* Anthroposophic Press, 2001.

—— *School as a Journey: The Eight-Year Odyssey of a Waldorf Teacher and His Class,* Anthroposophic Press, 1994.

Fenner, Pamela Johnson and Karen L. Rivers, eds. *Waldorf Student Reading List,* Michaelmas Press, 1995.

Fitzjohn, Sue, Minda Weston & Judy Large. *Festivals Together. A Guide to Multi-Cultural Celebration,* Hawthorn Press, 1993.

Franceschelli, Amos. *Mensuration: Mathematics for Grades 6, 7, and 8,* Mercury Press, 1985.

—— *Elementary Algebra,* Mercury Press, 1985.

Gabert, Erich. *Educating the Adolescent: Discipline or Freedom,* Anthroposophic Press, 1988.

—— *The Motherly and Fatherly Roles in Education,* Anthroposophic Press, 1977.

Gardner, John F. *Education in Search of the Spirit: Essays in American Education,* Anthroposophic Press, 1995.

—— *Youth Longs to Know: Explorations of the Spirit in Education,* Anthroposophic Press, 1997.

Glöckler, Michaela & Wolfgang Goebel. *A Guide to Child Health,* Floris Books, 2003.

Grohmann, Dr. Gerbert. *The Living World of the Plants,* The Association of Waldorf Schools of North America, 1999.

Haller, I. *How Children Play,* Floris Books, 1991.

Hansmann, Henning. *Education for Special Needs,* Floris Books, 1992.

Haren, Wil Van and Rudolf Kischnick. *Child's Play: Games for Life,* Hawthorn Press, 1995.

Harwood, A.C. *The Recovery of Man in Childhood: A Study in the Educational Work of Rudolf Steiner,* 2nd edition, Myrin Institute, 2001.

—— *The Way of a Child: An Introduction to the Work of Rudolf Steiner for Children,* Rudolf Steiner Press, 1967.

Hauschka, Rudolf. *Nutrition,* Rudolf Steiner Press, 1983.

—— *The Nature of Substance,* Rudolf Steiner Press, 1983.

Hemleben, Johannes. *Rudolf Steiner: An Illustrated Biography,* Rudolf Steiner Press, 2000.

Heydebrand, Caroline von. *Childhood: A Study of the Growing Child,* Anthroposophic Press, 1988.

Holdrege, Craig. *The Dynamic Heart and Circulation,* The Association of Waldorf Schools of North America, 2002.

Holtzapfel, Walter, M.D. *Children's Destinies: The Three Directions of Human Development,* Mercury Press, 1977.

—— *The Human Organs: Their Functional and Psychological Significance,* Lanthorn Press, 1993.

Hutchins, Eileen. *Parzival: An Introduction,* Temple Lodge Publishing, 1979.

Jaffke, Freya. *Work and Play in Early Childhood,* Anthroposophic Press, 1996.

—— *Toymaking with Children,* Floris Books, 2002.

James, Van. *Spirit and Art: Pictures of the Transformation of Consciousness,* Anthroposophic Press, 2001.

Jenkinson, Sally. *The Genius of Play: Celebrating the Spirit of Childhood,* Hawthorn Press, 2001.

Karutz, Matthais. *Forming School Communities: The Renewal of the Social Organism,* The Association of Waldorf Schools of North America, 2001.

Kirshner, *Dynamic Drawing: Its Therapeutic Aspects,* Mercury Press, 1977.

Kischnick, Rudolf. *Games, Gymnastics, Sport in Child Development,* Rudolf Steiner Press, 1979.

Klocek, Dennis. *Drawing from the Book of Nature,* Rudolf Steiner College Publications, 1990.

Kohler, Henning. *Working with Anxious, Nervous, and Depressed Children,* The Association of Waldorf Schools of North America, 2002.

König, Karl. *Brothers and Sisters: A Study in Child Psychology,* Floris Books, 1983.

—— *The First Three Years of the Child,* Anthroposophic Press, 1984.

—— *The Human Soul,* Anthroposophic Press, 1973.

Koepke, Hermann. *Encountering the Self: Transformation and Destiny in the Ninth Year,* Anthroposophic Press, 1989.

—— *On The Threshold of Adolescence,* Anthroposophic Press, 1992.

Kühlewind, Georg. *From Normal to Healthy: Paths to the Liberation of Consciousness,* Lindisfarne Press, 1988.

Kutzli, Rudolf. *Creative Form Drawing,* vols. 1, 2, 3, & 4, Hawthorn Press, 1983.

Lachman, Gary. *A Secret History of Consciousness,* Lindisfarne Books, 2003.

Large, Martin. *Set Free Childhood: Parents Survival Guide for Coping with Computers and TV,* Hawthorn Press, 2002.

Leeuwen, M.V. & J. Moeskops. *The Nature Corner,* Floris Books, 1990.

Lindenberg, Christoph. *Teaching History: Suggested Themes for the Curriculum in Waldorf Schools,* Association of Waldorf Schools of North America, 1989.

Lindenberg, Christoph-Andreas. *The Child's Praise of the Seasons: Festival Music to Sing,* Rose Harmony Association, 1995.

Lievegoed, Bernard. *Phases of Childhood,* Floris Books, 1987.

—— *Phases: Crisis and Development in the Individual,* Rudolf Steiner Press, 1979.

Lissau, Rudi. *Rudolf Steiner, Life, Work, Inner Path and Social Initiatives,* Hawthorn Press, 1987.

Logan, Arnold, arranged. & edited. *Building the Chorus: Exercises and Songs for All Voices,* Rose Harmony Association, 1994.

Luxford, Michael. *Adolescence and Its Significance for Those with Special Needs*, Camphill Books, 1995.

—— *Children with Special Needs: Rudolf Steiner's Ideas in Practice,* Anthroposophic Press, 1994.

Mackensen, Manfred von. *A Phenomena Based Physics,* 3 vols., Association of Waldorf Schools of North America, 1987.

Marshall, Ruth. *Celebrating Irish Festivals,* Hawthorn Press, 2003.

Matthews, Paul. *Sing Me the Creation.* Stroud, UK: Hawthorn Press, 1994.

McAllen, Audrey E. *The Extra Lesson: Exercises in Movement, Drawing and Painting for Helping Children in Difficulties with Writing, Reading and Arithmetic,* Steiner Schools Fellowship, 1985.

—— *Teaching Children to Write*, Rudolf Steiner Press, 1977.

McDermott, Robert. *The Essential Steiner: Basic Writings of Rudolf Steiner*, Lindisfarne Books, 2007.

Mees, L. F. C., M.D. *Living Metals: Relationship between Man and Metals*, Regency Press, 1974.

Mellon, Nancy. *Storytelling with Children*, Hawthorn Press, 2000.

Meyer, Rudolf. *Rhythms in Human Beings and the Cosmos*, Floris Books, 1985.

—— *The Wisdom of Fairy Tales*, Anthroposophic Press, 1981.

Mitchell, David & Patricia Livingston. *Will-Developed Intelligence: Handwork and Practical Arts in the Waldorf School*, The Association of Waldorf Schools of North America, 1999.

Müller, Brunhild. *Painting with Children*, Floris, 2002.

Murphy, Christine, ed. *The Vaccination Dilemma*, Lantern Books, 2002.

Neall, Lucinda. *Bringing Out the Best in Boys: Communication Strategies for Teachers*, Hawthorn Press, 2003.

Niederhauser, Hans R. & Margaret Frohlich. *Form Drawing*, Mercury Press, 1984.

Odent, Michel. *Primal Health*, Rudolf Steiner Press, Clairview Books, 2001.

Oldfield, Lynne. *Free to Learn: Introducing Steiner Waldorf Early Childhood Education*, Hawthorn Press, 2001.

O'Neill, George and Gisela. *The Human Life*. Florin Lowndes, ed., Mercury Press, 1990.

Pelikan, Wilhelm. *The Secrets of Metals*, Anthroposophic Press, 1973.

Petrash, Carol. *Earthways: Simple Environmental Activities for Young Children*, Gryphon Press, 1992.

Poplawski, Thomas, *Eurythmy: Rhythm, Dance and Soul*, Anthroposophic Press, 1998.

Pusch, Ruth, ed. *Waldorf Schools*, Vols. 1 & 2, Mercury Press, 1993.

Querido, René. *Creativity in Education: The Waldorf Approach*, H.S. Dalkin, 1984.

—— *The Esoteric Background of Waldorf Education: The Cosmic Christ Impulse*, Rudolf Steiner College Press, 1995.

—— *The Mystery of the Holy Grail: A Modern Path of Initiation*, Rudolf Steiner Press, 1991.

Rawson, Martyn & Michael Rose. *Ready to Learn,* Hawthorn Press, 2001.

Richards, Mary Caroline. *Opening Our Moral Eye: Essays, Talks, & Poems Embracing Creativity & Community,* Lindisfarne Press, 1995.

Schad, Wolfgang. *Man and Mammals: Toward a Biology of Form,* Garden City Waldorf Press, 1977.

Schmidt, Gerhard, M.D. *The Dynamics of Nutrition: The Impulse of Rudolf Steiner's Spiritual Science for a New Nutritional Hygiene,* Bio-Dynamic Literature, 1980.

—— *The Essentials of Nutrition,* Bio-Dynamic Literature, 1980.

Schmidt, Rudolf. *An English Grammar,* The Association of Waldorf Schools of North America, 1997.

Schwartz, Eugene. *Millennial Child: Transforming Education in the Twenty-first Century,* Anthroposophic Press, 1999.

—— *Gratitude, Love, and Duty: Their Unfolding in Waldorf Education,* Association for a Healing Education, 1989.

—— *Rhythms and Turning Points in the Life of the Child,* Rudolf Steiner College Publications, 1991.

—— *Seeing, Hearing, Learning: The Interplay of Eye and Ear in Waldorf Education,* Rudolf Steiner College Publications, 1990.

Schwenk, Theodor. *Sensitive Chaos: The Creation of Flowing Forms in Water and Air,* Rudolf Steiner Press, 1996.

—— *Water: The Element of Life,* Anthroposophic Press, 2002.

Sealey, Maricristin. *Kinder Dolls: A Waldorf Doll-Making Handbook,* Hawthorn Press, 2001.

Sheen, A. Renwick. *Geometry and the Imagination: The Imaginative Treatment of Geometry in Waldorf Education,* The Association of Waldorf Schools of North America, 2002.

Sleigh, Julian. *Thirteen to Nineteen: Discovering the Light: Conversations with Parents,* Floris Books, 1989.

Sloan, David. *Stages of Imagination: Working Dramatically with Adolescents,* The Association of Waldorf Schools of North America, 2001.

Smit, Jorgen. *Lighting Fires: Deepening Education Through Meditation,* Hawthorn Press, 1992.

—— *How to Transform Thinking, Feeling and Willing,* Hawthorn Press, 1989.

Smith, Edward Reaugh. *The Soul's Long Journey,* Anthroposophic Press, 2003.

Smith, Patti & Signe Eklund Schaeffer. *More Lifeways: Finding Support and Inspiration in Family Life,* Hawthorn Press, 1997.

Soesman, Albert. *Our Twelve Senses,* Hawthorn Press, 1998

Spock, Marjorie. *Eurythmy,* Anthroposophic Press, 1980.

—— *Teaching as a Lively Art,* Anthroposophic Press, 1978.

Staley, Betty. *Between Form and Freedom: A Practical Guide to the Teenage Years,* Hawthorn Press, 1988.

Stockmeyer, Karl E. A., *Rudolf Steiner's Curriculum for the Waldorf Schools,* Steiner Schools Fellowship, 1982.

Sussman, Linda. *Speech of the Grail: A Journey Toward Speaking that Heals and Transforms,* Lindisfarne Press, 1995.

Swanson, Herbert J. *Geometry for the Waldorf High School,* The Association of Waldorf Schools of North America, 1987.

Trostli, Roberto. *Rhythms of Learning: What Waldorf Education Offers Children, Parents, and Teachers,* Anthroposophic press, 1998.

—— *Physics is Fun! A Sourcebook for Teacher,* Octavo Editions, 1995.

Turgeniev, Assya. *Reminiscences of Rudolf Steiner,* Temple Lodge Publishing, 2003.

Vogt, Felicitas. *Addiction's Many Faces: Tackling Drug Dependency among Young People,* Hawthorn Press, 1999.

Whicher, Olive. *Projective Geometry,* Rudolf Steiner Press, 1971.

Wilkinson, Roy. *Rudolf Steiner: An Introduction to His Spiritual World-View,* Temple Lodge Publishing, 2002.

—— *The Spiritual Basis of Steiner Education,* Rudolf Steiner Press, 1996.

—— *Rudolf Steiner on Education: A Compendium,* Hawthorn Press, 1993.

Woodward, Bob & Marge Hogenboom. *Autism: A Holistic Approach,* Floris Books, 2000.

Zajonc, Arthur. *Catching the Light: The Entwined History of Light and Mind,* Bantam Books, 1993.

Zur Linden, Wilhelm. *A Child Is Born: Pregnancy, Birth and First Childhood,* Rudolf Steiner Press, 1973.